Assessing Outcomes and Improving Achievement
Tips and Tools for Using Rubrics

EDITED BY **Terrel L. Rhodes**

Association of American Colleges and Universities

Association of American Colleges and Universities
1818 R Street, NW, Washington, DC 20009
© 2010 by the Association of American Colleges and Universities
All rights reserved.

ISBN 978-0-911696-61-5

Chapter 2 contains material reprinted by permission from "What Is a Rubric?" *Assessment Update: Progress, Trends, and Practices in Higher Education* 21, no. 6 (2009).

The Association of American Colleges and Universities gratefully acknowledges the support of State Farm Companies Foundation and the Fund for Improvement of Post Secondary Education, of which 95 percent (or $2,450,372) was from federal funds, and 5 percent (or $125,000) was from nongovernment sources.

Photos courtesy of: Clark University; Southern Illinois University, Carbondale; Lawrence University; and Washington & Lee University

© **Mixed Sources**
Product group from well-managed forests, controlled sources and recycled wood or fiber
www.fsc.org   Cert no. BV-COC-961849
© 1996 Forest Stewardship Council
FSC

Contents

VALUE Advisory Board

RANDY BASS
Assistant Provost for Teaching and Learning Initiatives; Georgetown University

MARCIA BAXTER MAGOLDA
Distinguished Professor of Educational Leadership; Miami University, Ohio

VERONICA BOIX MANSILLA
Research Associate and Lecturer on Education; Harvard University

JOHNNELLA BUTLER
Provost; Spelman College

HELEN CHEN
Research Scientist; Stanford University

ARIANE HOY
Senior Program Officer; The Bonner Foundation

GEORGE KUH
Chancellor's Professor and Director, Center for Postsecondary Research; Indiana University Bloomington

PEGGY MAKI
Education Consultant; Peggy Maki Associates

MARCIA MENTKOWSKI
Director, Educational Research and Evaluation; Alverno College

GLORIA ROGERS
Associate Executive Director, Professional Services; ABET, Inc.

ROBERT STERNBERG
Dean of Arts and Sciences; Tufts University

KATHLEEN BLAKE YANCEY
Kellogg H. Hunt Professor of English; Florida State University

Acknowledgments

Assessing Outcomes and Improving Achievement: Tips and Tools for Using Rubrics is one of two publications that have emerged from the Valid Assessment of Learning in Undergraduate Education (VALUE) project, which is one component of AAC&U's Liberal Education and America's Promise (LEAP) initiative. Funding for the VALUE project was made available through a grant from the Fund for the Improvement of Postsecondary Education (FIPSE). Additional funding support was provided by the State Farm Companies Foundation. We are deeply appreciative of the support and assistance from our respective grant officers, Krish Mathur at FIPSE and Deborah Traskell at State Farm.

The VALUE project was guided by an outstanding advisory board whose members not only brought varied expertise and insight to the project, but also contributed to lively conversations and provided valuable guidance for the development, direction, and quality of the project process and results. The board included Randy Bass (Georgetown University), Johnnella Butler (Spelman College), Helen Chen (Stanford University), Ariane Hoy (the Bonner Foundation), George D. Kuh (Indiana University), Marcia Baxter Magolda (Miami University), Peggy Maki (education consultant), Veronica Boix Mansilla (Harvard University), Marcia Mentkowski (Alverno College), Gloria Rogers (ABET), Robert Sternberg (Tufts University), and Kathleen Blake Yancey (Florida State University).

In particular, we are forever indebted to the over one hundred faculty members, student affairs professionals, assessment specialists, and other colleagues who contributed many hours of their time as rubric development team members. This group of volunteers from across the country represented every institutional type, multiple disciplines and interdisciplinary areas, and various organizations and centers focused on specific outcome areas. The combination of experts and novices, assessment specialists, and classroom teachers strengthened the development of the ultimate version of the VALUE rubrics through eighteen months of drafting, testing, and redrafting the rubric language, criteria, and concepts.

As an integral part of the project, the following twelve "leadership campuses" tested the VALUE rubrics by using e-portfolios of student work to determine the usability of the rubrics for the assessment of learning: Alverno College, Bowling Green State University, City University of New York La Guardia Community College, College of San Mateo, George Mason University, Kapi'olani Community College, Portland State University, Rose-Hulman Institute of Technology, San Francisco State University, Spelman College, St. Olaf College, and the University of Michigan. During the rubric development process, almost one hundred additional colleges and universities tested one or more of the rubrics with their own students' work and provided feedback on the usability and usefulness of the rubrics in assessing the quality of student achievement.

None of the rubric development and testing could have been accomplished in this brief time frame without the expert, guiding, and relentless leadership of Wende Morgaine, the VALUE initiative manager. Wende coordinated the recruitment of the rubric development teams, the development process, the testing of the rubric drafts by campuses, the multiple revisions and retesting activities, and the final framing and posting of the rubrics on the AAC&U Web site. Her tireless energy, organizational skills, and ability to engage disparate individuals in a common enterprise were central to the realization of fifteen rubrics faculty and institutions can use both to assess student learning in its many dimensions and to communicate with colleagues and students about the terrain of their learning as they move through and among our campuses.

Finally, we thank the authors of this volume, who have provided a valuable road map for thinking about, implementing, and using the VALUE rubrics for the formative and summative assessment of learning on campuses. AAC&U's publications and editorial staff also have been collaborative and assiduous in supporting the realization of this publication.

Introduction

Terrel L. Rhodes

With the national spotlight focused on higher education and the development of public accountability reporting mechanisms, college and university campuses have been strongly encouraged or required to adopt some form of national testing as a measure of student learning. This push for accountability and transparency in higher education is driven by a sense that students in the United States are lagging behind students in other countries, and a resultant call for comparisons of student performance across campuses based on a score derived from one of a few national tests.

In 2007, as part of its Liberal Education and America's Promise initiative, the Association of American Colleges and Universities (AAC&U) embarked on a national project to determine whether there is an alternative to the prevailing push for a single score purported to represent learning for students and institutions. Is there a way for students to demonstrate their learning through the work they are asked to produce in the curriculum and cocurriculum, rather than through a snapshot test? Is it possible to capture liberal learning in all of its rich and varied dimensions? Is there a shared set of expectations for learning that individual faculty can use in the classroom, that can be aggregated for programmatic evaluation and sampled for institutional reporting? Can individual assignments and the resultant work be the means of demonstrating student learning throughout a student's educational pathway across and among different institutions? Can the shared expectations for learning be articulated so that students can use them to understand and make judgments about their own learning strengths and weaknesses? Can we recognize and honor the diversity of institutions and students while establishing a nationally shared set of broad, nuanced expectations for learning regardless of type of institution, mission, or location? Can we assess student learning in ways that actually provide faculty and students with information helpful to improve pedagogy and the development of learning over time as well as provide programs and institutions with summative information for reporting? In short, can the direction and assumptions of the national conversation on accountability and the assessment of student learning be changed?

Through the Valid Assessment of Learning in Undergraduate Education (VALUE) project, AAC&U has maintained that what students and faculty do through teaching and learning constitutes a most complex set of processes; that learning needs to occur across a broader set of outcomes than the current standardized tests measure; and that learning is developmental or emergent over time, progressing faster in some outcome areas than in others and becoming more complex and sophisticated as students move through their educational pathways.

Rubrics are the articulation of this progressively more robust learning. The challenge faced in the VALUE project was how to establish that rubrics can provide the assurance that regardless of where they teach—type of institution, part of the country, or mix of programs—faculty are indeed talking about the same outcomes and sharing the same expectations for learning. To meet this challenge, it was necessary for faculty members and academic professionals to articulate what liberal learning looks like at beginning, intermediate, and advanced levels of accomplishment (see appendix) for all the essential learning outcomes (see fig. 1).

To accomplish this, the project grounded the development of the VALUE rubrics in the work faculty and other colleagues had done over many years, drawing from the rubrics already developed by campus colleagues as they articulated learning expectations for their students. We know that for some outcomes there exist few rubrics or clearly articulated expectations, while for others there are many of both. By analyzing these existing rubrics, national VALUE rubric development teams of faculty members and academic professionals identified essential expectations and criteria that were shared across institutions. Although the specific language differed and the emphasis among criteria changed from college to college, the rubric development teams found clearly shared criteria for the achievement of learning at progressively more sophisticated levels of performance in each of the

---

TERREL L. RHODES *is vice president for quality, curriculum, and assessment at the Association of American Colleges and Universities.*

outcome areas. In some instances, the teams identified missing aspects of learning that needed to be incorporated into the rubrics in order to make them more complete; for example, one common aspect was that the criteria were very text-bound and not reflective of how students can demonstrate learning through visual, graphical, digital, or artistic modes of communication.

Over the course of the project, rubrics for fifteen liberal learning outcomes were developed by teams of faculty members and academic professionals from all types of higher education institutions across the country.[1] More than one hundred individuals contributed through the rubric development teams. The initial rubrics went through three rounds of drafting, testing (on more than one hundred campuses), and redrafting, which resulted in the final versions contained in the appendix.

The VALUE rubrics are conceived as broad, generic, institutional-level rubrics. Our vision is that colleges and universities will select the rubrics that reflect their own learning outcomes and use them to write local versions that are reflective of their own missions, cultures, and practices. The VALUE rubrics can be translated and elaborated for assessment and improvement at programmatic and course levels. Obviously, the national VALUE rubrics are not designed for use in assessing individual class assignments; such rubrics need to be more tailored, more descriptive of the discourse within which they reside. However, to the degree that enhanced rubrics for individual assignments or courses map or contain the essential, shared criteria and expectations of the VALUE rubrics, faculty can talk about learning within the national arena as well as the local context. The nesting of the core criteria for the outcomes—from the course level through programs to the institutional level—allows for confidence that learning at every level of analysis is shared, while providing sufficiently detailed information to focus individual improvement. The Center for Teaching, Learning, and Technology at Washington State

---

FIGURE 1. The Essential Learning Outcomes

Beginning in school, and continuing at successively higher levels across their college studies, students should prepare for twenty-first-century challenges by gaining:

KNOWLEDGE OF HUMAN CULTURES AND THE PHYSICAL AND NATURAL WORLD
- Through study in the sciences and mathematics, social sciences, humanities, histories, languages, and the arts

Focused by engagement with big questions, both contemporary and enduring

INTELLECTUAL AND PRACTICAL SKILLS, INCLUDING
- Inquiry and analysis
- Critical and creative thinking
- Written and oral communication
- Quantitative literacy
- Information literacy
- Teamwork and problem solving

Practiced extensively, across the curriculum, in the context of progressively more challenging problems, projects, and standards for performance

PERSONAL AND SOCIAL RESPONSIBILITY, INCLUDING
- Civic knowledge and engagement—local and global
- Intercultural knowledge and competence
- Ethical reasoning and action
- Foundations and skills for lifelong learning

Anchored through active involvement with diverse communities and real-world challenges

INTEGRATIVE AND APPLIED LEARNING, INCLUDING
- Synthesis and advanced accomplishment across general and specialized studies

Demonstrated through the application of knowledge, skills, and responsibilities to new settings and complex problems

Source: Association of American Colleges and Universities, *College Learning for the New Global Century: A Report from the National Leadership Council for Liberal Education and America's Promise* (Washington, DC: Association of American Colleges and Universities), 12.

---

1   Rubrics were developed for all of AAC&U's essential learning outcomes except for those listed under the heading "Knowledge of Human Cultures and the Physical and Natural World," for which many measures already exist.

University has a well-developed set of examples of how general rubrics can be translated into programmatic and course rubrics and still supply useful feedback and assessment information for course, programmatic, and institutional purposes.[2]

The VALUE rubrics included in the appendix are also available on the AAC&U Web site at www.aacu.org/value/rubrics. There, for each rubric, we provide a definition of the outcome, framing language that explains the approach of the development team, a glossary of terms, the essential criteria for meeting the outcome from the most complex to the least complex demonstration of learning, and examples of student work that illustrate how in one instance the rubric was used to arrive at an assessment conclusion about student achievement for a specific criterion and outcome. The student work samples, in particular, are not intended to be exemplars, but rather to show how a piece of work demonstrated for a set of reviewers the level of performance for the specific criterion.

The performance levels reflected in the VALUE rubrics—capstone, milestones, and benchmark—do not represent year in school (freshman, sophomore …), nor do they correspond to grades (A, B, C …). Rather, the capstone level reflects the demonstration of achievement for the specific criterion for a student who graduates with a baccalaureate degree. Milestones suggest key characteristics of progressive learning as students move from early in their college experience to the completion of the baccalaureate degree. A benchmark performance reflects the learning skills and abilities of students our faculty team members found among their beginning college students. The rubrics do not represent college readiness standards. Our expectation is that campuses and individuals will not only adapt the VALUE rubrics to their own missions, cultures, and practices, but also develop their own versions of the rubrics by examining the work of their own students.

In sum, we are engaged in nothing less than an effort to change the focus of the national conversation from artificial, shorthand indicators of learning to something that reflects the shared work and understanding of faculty members and academic professionals across campuses. The VALUE project has demonstrated that the academy shares similar expectations and criteria for accomplishment on a broad range of learning outcomes. When we grade a paper, when we evaluate student performance, when we examine a program of study, or when we look at the graduates of an institution, we expect fundamentally similar levels of learning for our students. The VALUE rubrics represent the learning expectations broadly shared by faculty members and academic professionals across the country. Individual campuses will write local rubrics that reflect their institutional mission, program mix, and types of students and that use the appropriate language and detail to enable assessment at various levels; however, these local rubrics will still contain the essential criteria and expectations of learning that are shared broadly and expressed in the VALUE rubrics. In this way, we can all have confidence that, when we talk about learning, we are speaking a common language with shared standards that reflect the richness and complexity of the teaching and learning that actually occur on our campuses.

Assessing Outcomes and Improving Achievement: Tips and Tools for Using Rubrics explains how the VALUE project approached the work of drafting rubrics as well as frames an approach that individual campuses can use to build on from what has already been developed.

> We are engaged in nothing less than an effort to change the focus of the national conversation from artificial, shorthand indicators of learning to something that reflects the shared work and understanding of faculty members and academic professionals across campuses.

---

2   See wsuctlt.wordpress.com/2009/01/20/harvesting_gradebook.

CHAPTER 1:

Assessment of the Academy, for the Academy, by the Academy

Antonia J. Levi and Dannelle D. Stevens

What does it mean to be an educated person? How can we teach our students to become educated persons? How can we know whether we've succeeded? These questions have been bruited around college and university campuses for generations, but only in the past twenty years or so have they begun to be translated into action as faculty and administrators struggle to isolate the components of what we mean by "an educated person," and to assess whether an institution is, in fact, producing that desired result. For the most part, however, these efforts have been campus-specific. By working with a wide variety of campuses that already use rubrics for these purposes, the Valid Assessment of Learning in Undergraduate Education (VALUE) project of the Association of American Colleges and Universities (AAC&U) has produced an approach to defining and assessing student learning at the national level that is based on the values and practices of the academy itself.

Rubrics, after all, originate in the classroom. Initially a simple grading tool, rubrics are now being used by an increasing number of professors for the more complex task of evaluating student portfolios and even entire programs. Intended to reflect not only individual assignments but also progress in learning, a student portfolio for even a single class may contain a large number of different components that must be identified and then charted by the evaluator in a fair and consistent manner. Assessing such portfolios is no easy task, and many faculty members have turned to rubrics of one sort or another that spell out the various tasks they want their students to master, as well as the criteria for determining whether and to what degree students have actually succeeded in mastering them.

To assess entire programs or even entire campuses, randomly selected student work can be evaluated using the same method. Through the VALUE project, faculty and staff representatives from campuses that already engage in some form of rubric-based assessment have produced fifteen rubrics that represent a surprisingly consistent answer to the question, what does it mean to be an educated person?

HERDING CATS?

Administrators often bemoan the difficulty of getting faculty to agree on anything. It's like herding cats, they say, and many faculty themselves echo this sentiment. Yet while this may be true when it comes to campus politics, it is far less true of faculty views on the nature of education and what it means to be an educated person. On these points, faculty are in remarkable agreement. And that agreement quickly becomes apparent when groups of faculty work together to produce a rubric, whether for evaluating student work or for assessing entire programs.

In an experiment conducted in 2002, for example, six instructors involved in teaching an interdisciplinary freshman core set out to create a single grading rubric for a book critique assigned to their various classes. Despite the fact that the team included two English professors, an anthropologist, a historian, a chemist, and even a high school teacher offering the class as an Advanced Placement option, there was remarkably little disagreement regarding the performance criteria to be included in the rubric. Nor was there much variation in how the different instructors used the rubric to assess student work; the scores assigned were remarkably consistent. And when, as part of the experiment, outside evaluators were given a random selection of the book critiques, they produced scores similar to those given by the instructors. Such results are reassuring to instructors who often wonder whether their evaluations are consistent, fair, and in line with the practices of their colleagues. But they also reveal the common assumptions, expectations, and values that underlie the academy, as well as the ways in which rubrics can be used to reinforce and define them.

ANTONIA J. LEVI *is retired professor of Japanese history and popular culture, and* **DANNELLE D. STEVENS** *is professor of curriculum and instruction, both at Portland State University. They are the authors of* Introduction to Rubrics: An Assessment Tool to Save Grading Time, Convey Effective Feedback and Promote Student Learning *(Stylus, 2005).*

These commonalities still hold true when rubric construction is extended to program assessment, especially if and when faculty are involved in creating the rubrics by which their own programs are to be assessed. Involving faculty in this way ensures that the criteria are consistent with the values of both the academy in general and the program or institution in particular. Moreover, many individual faculty members find such involvement both empowering and enlightening. "I never really spelled out my teaching goals before," said one professor after working on a critical-thinking rubric for his department. "I guess I knew what I wanted to teach, but I'd never put it into words. Doing that and being able to discuss it with other department members really taught me a lot, and knowing we mostly agreed on what was important was pretty reassuring, too."

Professors who examine the VALUE rubrics will no doubt feel the same mix of enlightenment and reassurance. Few will find the concepts alien. Surely critical thinking, inquiry and analysis, creative thinking, written communication, and problem solving are among the skills that all faculty hope their students will achieve. Quantitative literacy, informational literacy, and teamwork represent more recent expectations for the educated person of the twenty-first century. And who could possibly argue with mastery of integrative learning or the foundations and skills for lifelong learning as a goal that stretches beyond the academy and into students' lives?

More controversial are the goals associated with personal and social responsibility, especially civic knowledge and engagement, intercultural knowledge and competence, and ethical reasoning. Some professors continue to insist that their students' ethical worldviews, however important they may be for daily life, are not related to their academic disciplines. The VALUE rubrics probably will not change this view overnight. Nonetheless, most will agree that the ability to articulate one's "own ethical values and the social context of problems," as it is described in the ethical-reasoning rubric, is relevant to almost all academic disciplines. Similarly, most will recognize as attributes of an educated person the ability to "articulate insights into [one's] own cultural rules and biases," the ability to "ask complex questions about other cultures," and the ability to "seek out and articulate answers to questions that reflect multiple cultural perspectives"—all of which are described in the intercultural knowledge and competence rubric.

> The VALUE rubrics reflect the emphasis the academy places on the ability to analyze and integrate knowledge in a variety of ways.

Indeed, these particular examples demonstrate perhaps better than anything else the difference between assessment measures based on external models (e.g., standardized tests) and those created within the academy. While the former focus on easily quantifiable measures such as content, the VALUE rubrics reflect the emphasis the academy places on the ability to analyze and integrate knowledge in a variety of ways. The academy is not unconcerned with content, of course. Professors of chemistry or history, for example, certainly want their students to learn some very specific content, but they also want them to display the ability to use that content in the ways reflected in the VALUE rubrics.

OUT OF THE CLASSROOM AND BACK AGAIN

As external pressures for accountability mount, in order to avoid having inappropriate assessment techniques foisted upon it, the academy must respond with the assessment techniques that are best suited to it. As far as their own campuses are concerned, the institutions involved in creating the VALUE rubrics have already taken steps in that direction. By gathering representatives from these institutions together to produce rubrics for national use, AAC&U has not only produced assessment tools that are especially well suited to the academy, but it has also begun to change the national dialogue on assessment and accountability.

For institutional purposes, some colleges and universities will find that they can use the VALUE rubrics as they stand. Because they were created by scholars from widely differing disciplines and institutional types, the rubrics are in fact quite universal. Other campuses, however, will want to use the VALUE rubrics as templates that can be altered to reflect specific concerns. Religious colleges, for example, may want to add to the essentially secular language of the ethical-reasoning rubric, while institutes of technology may want to make their criteria relate more closely to mathematics and the sciences. Hopefully, individual colleges and universities will make such alterations by following the same process used to create the original VALUE rubrics—that is, by gathering together representative members of their own faculties to discuss the original rubrics and how they should be altered. This method will not only produce rubrics that best reflect the individual campuses, but it will also involve professors in rubric construction.

Direct professorial involvement often has a side benefit for students. Professors who become involved in rubric construction as part of assessment practices are more likely to start translating rubrics for use in evaluating student work in their own classes. This use of rubrics—their original use—has great value for students because it spells out for them what it means to be an educated person, and rubrics offer regular milestones by which students can gauge their own progress. This is useful for all students, but it is particularly so for nontraditional students—nonnative speakers of English, international students, students who are the first in their families to go to college, and students who, for whatever reason, are less well attuned to the culture and expectations of the American academy. Such students are an increasing presence on college campuses, and anything that helps them find their way in this (to them) unfamiliar environment is to be welcomed.

> Rubrics offer regular milestones by which students can gauge their own progress.

CONCLUSION

Few people question the need to assess college and university programs in order to ensure that they are actually doing what they set out to do, namely, to produce educated persons. Yet many professors are hostile to assessment efforts. There are several reasons for this hostility, but one is undoubtedly the fact that the methodologies of too many assessment efforts are drawn from other kinds of institutions—most commonly corporate—and are seldom appropriate to the goals of the academy. By contrast, the VALUE project has developed a methodology drawn from the practices of the academy itself and attuned to its distinctive goals.

CHAPTER 2:

What is a Rubric?

Merilee Griffin

A rubric is not a technical specification, like how to build a bridge. Nor is it a checklist for ailing student performances in need of therapy. It is certainly not a Gotcha Grid for wayward writers. It is not even, as Merriam Webster said, an authoritative rule, although it meant that at one time.

When it was first born into the English language, "rubric" meant the color red, because monks passing their lives away in medieval monasteries, beautifully hand-copying their Latin texts, used red ink for headings. The word spent the next thousand years or so meaning "heading," and gradually its mission crept to include "classification."

Old issues of *College English* contain many uses of the word "rubric" as a heading or classification, including this one from a 1962 article called "An Existential Examination of King Lear":

> This new humility is in remarkable contrast to the old arrogance. Under this general rubric of human relations, the tragedy of King Lear can be seen as a profound study of the nature of evil (Vol. 23, Issue 7, p. 548).

And then in the October 1981 issue, the word occurs in an article called "The Validity of the Advanced Placement English Language and Composition Examination." For the first time, it has something to do with scoring:

> The readers were trained to score the essays holistically, considering their overall quality, form, and content together. They used a nine-point scale and were guided by a scoring guide or "rubric."

The appended rubric seems old-fashioned and vague compared with the matrices we are accustomed to now. It begins:

> General Directions: Reward the essays for what they do well in response to the question. After you have read an essay and determined its score, you may raise that score one point if the essay is very well written. A badly written essay must be given a score no higher than four.

The tone suggests we may be invited to tea following the session.

Since then, the scoring rubric has evolved into a more precise, technical, scientific-looking document. It carries a tone of certainty, authority, and exactitude. That facade is deceptive, however, because a rubric is more like a cake than a rock. It contains whatever we put in it, not what nature designed. Different people like different kinds of cake, and there are many ways to bake them. So what is a rubric?

A rubric is the creation of the people who made it rather than a mirror reflection of some permanent and absolute reality.

A rubric is a series of choices. Unfortunately, like a phone booth, it can be stuffed with only so many bodies. Some things have to be left out, because if we included everything it would have to be printed in eight-point type on a bed sheet. So we choose the things we think are most important, at least for our particular students, at this point in their lives. The hard part is that our students are all over the map in their skill levels and their linguistic and intellectual needs. Still, the rubric is our best judgment about what matters most in the stage of human development we think our students are currently in.

> A rubric is the creation of the people who made it rather than a mirror reflection of some permanent and absolute reality.

MERILEE GRIFFIN *is research coordinator for the Tier I Writing Assessment at Michigan State University and an affiliate of the Center for Writing in a Digital Environment. She is also president of Collaborative Online Assessments, a nonprofit organization advocating the fusion of authentic assessment, technology, and faculty development (www.coassess.org). This chapter is reprinted by permission from "What Is a Rubric?" Assessment Update: Progress, Trends, and Practices in Higher Education 21, no. 6 (2009).*

A rubric is an uneasy balance between generality and specificity. We want every statement to be general enough to encompass all the things we value, but it must be specific enough to spell out our meanings.

A rubric is one of the most carefully written documents in history. The signers of the Declaration of Independence could not have spent more time haggling over words than most committees charged with creating a rubric. Every member morphs into a lawyer, a judge, and a philologist with thesaurus in hand, and every word is dissected and analyzed before it is included.

A rubric is the record of negotiated compromises, the lingering detritus of struggles for dominance by purists and poets and pragmatists. In these contests, some win and some lose. No one gets everything they want and everybody gets a little something. The rubric is the final scorecard.

The rubric is a product of many minds working collaboratively to create new knowledge. It will, almost by definition, be more thoughtful, valid, unbiased, and useful than any one of us could have conceived of working in isolation. The discussions that haven't killed it have made it stronger.

The rubric is not a universal statement of truth for the ages. Like the Constitution, it is a living document that must change with the times. It should change a bit slowly, only when someone cares enough to mount a serious challenge to the status quo. The rubric will have to become a pretty bad match for our needs before we stop complaining about it and do something, but eventually we will.

Ultimately, our rubric is the very best of our collective professional and intellectual selves at this little point in time, in our small spot on the planet. It is the finest description of what we think is important for our students, right now, in the service of their learning. Most importantly, it is a statement of our mutual commitment to be guided by the highest and most carefully considered values in our professional practice. It is what we promise to teach.

> **Our rubric is a statement of our mutual commitment to be guided by the highest and most carefully considered values in our professional practice. It is what we promise to teach.**

CHAPTER 3:
Developing Rubrics: Lessons Learned

Wende Morgaine

The emphasis on assessment at colleges and universities across the country has created a need not just for assessment tools, but for tools that can yield meaningful information about student learning, experiences, and success. In response, many campuses have appointed committees, often comprised of faculty members, to create or redesign existing assessment tools. Increasingly, however, these efforts have sought to evaluate student achievement at the programmatic level as well as at the level of individual courses.

And although faculty can expertly evaluate the work assigned within a particular course, they are less accustomed to creating assessment tools that span both program objectives and subject matter such that student learning and success can be measured both within *and* across college curricula. To do this, faculty must learn to conduct assessment not only within a group but also *as a group*; they must share knowledge, reflect upon expected outcomes, build consensus, and take collective ownership of the assessment.

> Faculty must learn to conduct assessment not only within a group but also *as a group*; they must share knowledge, reflect upon expected outcomes, build consensus, and take collective ownership of the assessment.

The Valid Assessment of Learning in Undergraduate Education (VALUE) project of the Association of American Colleges and Universities (AAC&U) typifies how, using rubrics, faculty can work collectively to create meaningful assessment of student learning. Over the course of eighteen months, fifteen teams of faculty, administrators, and other academic professionals from around the country created rubrics to assess the essential learning outcomes identified through AAC&U's Liberal Education and America's Promise initiative (see fig. 1, p. 2). In addition to producing the rubrics themselves, the rubric development process created a road map of sorts for the process of creating rubrics as a group. What follows are the lessons learned through the VALUE project.

DON'T REINVENT THE WHEEL

Departments and institutions often have assessment tools with which they are already working. This is not to say that they don't need to create local versions of the VALUE rubrics, versions tailored to particular contexts, but rather that the local process doesn't need to reinvent the entire wheel. Local rubric development groups should begin by searching for existing examples of assessments, and then proceed by discussing how these examples might be adapted to meet departmental or institutional objectives.

For each of fifteen learning outcomes, the VALUE project collected approximately twenty sample rubrics from campuses around the country. This early rubric collection is located online and can be searched by subject area (see openedpractices.org). Anyone in higher education may add resources to the site or use it as a public library for local rubric development projects.

Once the rubrics for an outcome area were collected (primarily through Internet searches for publicly posted material and contributions from individual faculty), they were shared with each of the rubric development teams. The teams then examined the rubrics and identified the common criteria found most frequently across each collection. These criteria became the foundation of the VALUE rubrics.

For some less common outcomes—for example, integrative learning, civic engagement, and creative thinking—fewer rubrics were available. In these instances, the teams utilized other important sources identified by faculty from the relevant fields to determine the criteria on which there appeared to be widespread agreement within a discipline or learning outcome area.

WENDE MORGAINE *is manager of the Valid Assessment of Learning in Undergraduate Education (VALUE) project at the Association of American Colleges and Universities. For more information about rubric development for your campus, contact her at value@aacu.org.*

MANY HANDS MAKE LIGHT WORK

Both the size and the composition of a team can affect the achievement of rubric development goals. After working on the VALUE project with teams of varying sizes, we concluded that a team of five to ten people is optimal. Teams of this size were able to continue working when one or two people needed to miss a meeting. Smaller teams were not always able to gather enough members at one time to advance the work, and as a result they encountered more delays than the larger teams.

In terms of composition, it is important for the end users of the assessment rubric to be represented on the committee or team responsible for developing it. For example, if the rubric is intended for use across a department where faculty are divided into different theoretical camps, a representative from each camp should be included on the team. If the rubric is to be used across disciplines, an interdisciplinary team is vital. It is also important to remember that students themselves are end users, which makes attention to the clarity of terms and simplicity of language an essential component of rubric development. In the VALUE project, the teams with greater diversity in terms of the range of disciplines represented by the team members were able more easily to create accessible and understandable final rubrics. Their ability to draw from different disciplines and perspectives made it easier for them to write for students while addressing the content and academic standards each outcome demanded.

BEGIN WITH THE END IN MIND

Starting the rubric development process with a blank page can sometimes result in an end product that is so detailed and comprehensive that it is difficult for end users to implement it; the rubric will likely lack conciseness, a component key to both adoptability and adaptability. To develop a rubric that is both thorough and concise, it is useful for groups to start the development process with a few guidelines based on what is ultimately needed. For example, from the beginning, the VALUE project limited the number of performance levels in the rubrics as well as the number of criteria. Individual teams were able to meet these limits by forcing themselves, as individuals and as a group, to determine the most vital criteria for each outcome. Of course, the limits can always be expanded should feedback indicate that a rubric is too narrow. But only rarely did the rubric development teams receive that type of feedback from colleagues who tested the rubrics. The single, most common piece of feedback received (from over one hundred colleges and universities) during the VALUE process was that the rubrics should be made "shorter, more concise, simpler." Since it is often easier to expand than to cut, doing the hard work of being concise early will likely save the group time later on.

THE PROOF IS IN THE PUDDING

When creating a rubric, there is always a certain amount of hesitancy in actually putting something on the page. Academics are sometimes more comfortable with a comprehensive discussion of the philosophical implications of one focus for assessment versus another. But this dimension of rubric creation can often lead to a long, frustrating process that can take years to produce even the first draft of a rubric. Beginning with this type of discussion is doubly undesirable when the campus need for rubrics is immediate.

The challenge, then, is to put something on paper and to test it. Progress only results from actually *doing something*. Teams shouldn't be afraid to release a first draft with the understanding that it will probably be revised substantially. One strategy that helped move the rubrics onto paper in the VALUE project was to apportion the work. Each member of every rubric development team was responsible for one criterion, and she or he wrote performance descriptors for each of the four levels of a particular VALUE rubric (see the appendix for examples). Just one criterion per team member was a manageable workload. But since this was an assignment given to each rubric development team member *very* early in the process, there were draft rubrics on paper almost immediately. Teams then devoted time to discussing each sentence, and often each word, in terms of its implications for a field or its effect on student work. By that point, the teams were discussing and editing an actual product. The discussion was no longer theoretical. The goal of drafting a rubric had been accomplished, and what remained was the detailed process of revision.

The VALUE process worked because, by getting something on paper early, each team had, in essence, made a prototype that could be tested and retested. One team member used the analogy of making pudding: "A discussion about how to make pudding is only useful for so long. In the end, you have to mix ingredients and do taste tests if you want to make good pudding."

KICK THE TIRES

Once you have something on paper, you need people to test it and to provide feedback. Testing and feedback are crucial for creating quality assessment tools, and it is especially important that the feedback be meaningful. Too often, the people recruited to offer feedback assume they should passively *read* the tool without applying its content. In the VALUE project, we found that actually *testing* the rubrics *on student work* was essential to the creation of useful rubrics. Feedback was always based on testing. It's the same difference between looking at a car and actually driving it. This step was indispensable for both the feedback volunteers and the rubric development teams. Whenever the teams tested the rubrics with student work, they wrote better, more specific performance descriptors.

To achieve high-quality feedback, it is strongly recommended that at least two or three feedback and revision cycles be built into the rubric creation process. In the VALUE project, every rubric was tested and revised at least twice. Some rubrics were tested and revised three times. We found consistently that it was these later revision cycles that generated the type and diversity of feedback needed to increase significantly the quality of the rubrics.

CAST A WIDE NET

Obtain feedback from as many people as possible. Asking a large number of people to give feedback will help build buy-in for the assessment itself, while also providing input from diverse perspectives. A key element of the VALUE project was that the number of campuses providing feedback was increased for each feedback cycle. We started with twelve campuses in the first feedback cycle, and by the end over one hundred campuses had tested the rubrics.

Additionally, starting with a small amount of feedback in the first testing and feedback cycle can be helpful. The initial testing of the first three VALUE rubrics enabled the project both to revise the rubrics and to tweak the development process for the remaining twelve rubrics. These tweaks made the process more efficient and also helped make the first drafts of the remaining twelve rubrics much stronger.

In some cases, this approach might require teams to seek feedback not only from colleagues on campus, but also from those at other institutions across the country, or even around the world, who are in the discipline or field for which the rubric is being designed. Teams might also want to consider inviting community members to participate in the testing and to provide additional feedback. One lesson learned points to the value of involving colleagues from the cocurricular side of the institution. Their insight into how students might perceive a rubric was invaluable as the VALUE rubrics were being created.

> Testing and feedback are crucial for creating quality assessment tools, and it is especially important that the feedback be meaningful.

Ultimately, the goal of seeking feedback from multiple sources is to be able to identify universal or common themes. In the VALUE project, for example, the need to simplify jargon for student readers and the importance of limiting each performance descriptor to a single, measurable behavior emerged as common themes. Whenever a theme could reasonably be applied to all rubrics, it was. Looking for the common themes in feedback is central to helping identify fruitful directions for revision. In the VALUE process, trying to respond to each piece of specific feedback often sent the teams in contradictory directions; but in responding to the common themes from the feedback, teams found that the revisions always improved the quality of the rubrics.

CONCLUSION

The process of creating assessment rubrics can be both challenging and enlightening for any campus. Almost without exception, the rubric development team members in the VALUE project spoke of the many benefits of their participation in the rubric creation and revision process in terms of their own teaching and scholarship. Although daunting, the process of creating and revising assessment rubrics is a rewarding one for faculty and a fruitful one for institutions.

CHAPTER 4:

How Do I Use Rubrics to Evaluate Student Work?

Rowanna L. Carpenter

Many campuses do not have experience in developing and using rubrics to assess student work, and many of the faculty and staff who participated in the Valid Assessment of Learning in Undergraduate Education (VALUE) project sought advice on how to utilize rubrics to conduct valid and reliable reviews of student learning. Portland State University, one of the twelve original institutions that agreed to test the VALUE rubrics with student work on its campus, has for over a decade been using rubrics systematically for course and program review. The effective use of rubrics to evaluate student work, as described below, can be adapted to a multitude of circumstances, regardless of the specific design or focus a campus may have for assessing learning.

Portland State University has used a portfolio review process to assess and monitor student learning in general education since 1994. During that time, student portfolios have moved from a paper to an electronic format, and students' final portfolios are now developed entirely online. These student e-portfolios provide valuable evidence of learning during students' first year in the general education program.

INSTITUTIONAL CONTEXT

Portland State is a large, public research university located in the heart of Portland, Oregon. In the fall of 2008, Portland State enrolled 26,382 students, of whom 20,515 were undergraduates. A new general education program called University Studies was adopted in 1994, after a faculty committee reformed the previous distribution-model program. University Studies is a four-level program, extending throughout a students' time at Portland State. The curriculum is inquiry based and structured around four goals: communication, critical thinking, the diversity of human experience, and ethics and social responsibility. E-portfolios are used in Freshman Inquiry (FRINQ), the program's yearlong first-year requirement. The FRINQ curriculum is based on themes designed by interdisciplinary teams of faculty—for example, The Work of Art, Cyborg Millennium, or Design and Society.

THE FRESHMAN INQUIRY E-PORTFOLIO

The FRINQ e-portfolio is a common assignment across all FRINQ courses that requires students to reflect on their learning over the course of the year and to select and discuss two pieces of evidence of their learning related to each of the four University Studies goals. As a course-based assignment, the e-portfolio is a graded part of the FRINQ course. The direct evidence of student learning provided by these e-portfolios is also used for program-level assessment.

UNIVERSITY STUDIES RUBRICS

FRINQ e-portfolios are assessed using locally developed, holistic rubrics related to each of the four goals. Each rubric employs a six-point scale to represent the range of a student's learning, from freshman (levels 1, 2, and 3) to senior (level 5 or 6) year. The rubrics were developed by teams of faculty, including faculty teaching in University Studies as well as a range of other faculty from across Portland State University. In 2007, the FRINQ coordinator and the assessment coordinator created a checklist inventory of the types of assignments students have to include in their e-portfolios. This inventory provided supplemental information that helped contextualize the e-portfolio scoring.

UNIVERSITY STUDIES E-PORTFOLIO REVIEW

E-portfolio selection. Before e-portfolios are selected for review, informed consent is obtained from students enrolled in FRINQ classes—the students complete an online consent form during mentor sessions, a process approved by the Institutional Review Board. Over the last three years, the response rate has ranged between

ROWANNA L. CARPENTER *is assessment coordinator for University Studies at Portland State University.*

60 and 80 percent, with approximately 70–75 percent of students each year giving their consent. In the spring of 2009, just over six hundred students consented to have their e-portfolios reviewed as part of the assessment process.

A random sample of thirty e-portfolios per theme (or a total of 210 e-portfolios) is reviewed. To select these e-portfolios, the students who gave consent are divided into their respective thematic groups. Each student in these groups is assigned a random number, and the thirty assigned the lowest numbers in each group are selected for review. Once students have been selected, their faculty members are asked to send e-portfolio URLs to the assessment coordinator.

Reviewer recruitment. To review the 210 e-portfolios each year, the University Studies program hires approximately forty reviewers, including faculty both within the program and across the campus as well as graduate students. During the middle of spring term, a recruitment notice is posted in the campuswide weekly newsletter and also is sent via e-mail to academic department chairs and faculty who teach in the University Studies program. Each year faculty representing as many departments as possible are hired, and graduate students from programs across campus supplement the reviewer group. As an incentive to participate, faculty and graduate students are paid a small stipend and are provided coffee and lunch on the days of the review. No problems have occurred in using this approach to recruit reviewers.

The use of such a broad approach to reviewer recruitment is an intentional choice. Faculty who do not teach in University Studies are able to see the kind of work being done by students and faculty in the general education program. Similarly, faculty who teach at the capstone (senior) level of the University Studies program are given a glimpse of the types of learning experiences students gain as they begin their studies. And the use of outside reviewers to assess student work contributes to program transparency.

E-portfolio review. Each year, the University Studies program focuses on two of its four goals during e-portfolio review, dedicating one day of review to each goal. The review takes place during the week between the spring and summer terms. We have found this to be a time when faculty can dedicate a whole day to the review, which is preferable to breaking up the day as they leave to teach classes. Also, because the review takes place in the computer labs used for mentor sessions, it is most convenient to schedule it for a time when classes are not in session and the labs are not in use.

All reviewers convene early in the day for a welcome and training session. Because faculty are recruited from outside of University Studies, the day begins with an introduction to the program and its goals. An overview of FRINQ and the e-portfolios is also provided. After the brief introduction, the procedures for using a rubric to score student e-portfolios are reviewed, with an emphasis on the need to compare student work with the rubric criteria—not other e-portfolios and not other criteria. For example, when the criterion reviewed is diversity or ethics and social responsibility, it is pointed out that a student's use of grammar is not relevant and should not figure in reviewers' scoring decisions. It is stressed that reviewers must use the rubric as it is currently constructed and that comments about how it might be changed will be taken at the end of the day.

Following the orientation session, reviewers read the rubric of the day and apply it to a test e-portfolio. All reviewers score the same e-portfolio and then reconvene to discuss their scores. The reviewers then report their scores, which are tallied on a board to give a sense of whether they are clustering around one or two points on the rubric (the goal of calibration). If some reviewers give scores that lie outside the main cluster, they are asked to explain them in relation to the rubric criteria. Next, a reviewer whose score falls within the majority cluster is asked to explain his or her score. This discussion continues until agreement is reached about how to score the e-portfolios. Then the reviewers review a second test e-portfolio, and a similar conversation follows. When there is consensus about how to score, reviewers are left to score e-portfolios for the rest of the day.

Each e-portfolio is reviewed by at least two reviewers. If the two initial scores are the same or differ by one point, then the mean of the two scores is assigned as the final e-portfolio score. If the two scores differ by more than one point—for example, if one reviewer assigns a two and the other assigns a four—then a third person reviews the e-portfolio. If the third score converges with either of the first two scores, then the mean of those two scores is taken. If the third score differs by more than one point, then a conference is called and the three reviewers meet to determine the final score. As a way to monitor the scoring process, scores are recorded on a spreadsheet, and e-portfolios that need third reviews are flagged.

At the end of the day, the reviewers gather again and are given a chance to offer feedback on both the process and the rubric. It is very helpful to hear from reviewers about their experience using the rubrics and about areas that may be confusing. These comments have helped improve and clarify the rubrics over the years. This session also provides feedback about the e-portfolio assignment itself.

Processing and using the data. The data generated through this e-portfolio review process are used in two ways. First, aggregate means and frequencies are generated across all the e-portfolio scores. These data allow for the monitoring of program performance over time. Second, the scores are aggregated by theme and provided to the faculty teams. The teams use these data to identify areas for improvement, and the resulting improvements are subsequently incorporated into the course curricula. Faculty discuss the e-portfolio findings at a fall retreat before the beginning of the academic year. The e-portfolio data have informed improvements in the way writing is taught in freshman inquiry and have helped identify quantitative literacy as an area in need of additional focus. The e-portfolio review process has also resulted in the adjustment of the e-portfolio assignment over time to outline program expectations of students more clearly.

CHAPTER 5:

A Guide for How Faculty Can Get Started Using the VALUE Rubrics

Linda Adler-Kassner, Carol Rutz, and Susanmarie Harrington

For many faculty members and academic and student affairs professionals, using rubrics to score or evaluate student achievement of learning outcomes is venturing into a new arena. The preceding chapters describe processes and strategies for organizing campus work that can enhance assessment for learning. Through the process developed through the Valid Assessment of Learning in Undergraduate Education (VALUE) project, we have discovered that the development and use of rubrics with collections of student work can have several key benefits:

- Rubrics help faculty articulate more precisely what the learning they want their students to achieve actually looks like.
- Rubrics help students understand the expectations for their learning.
- Rubrics reinforce assessment for learning, not just assessment of learning.
- Rubrics place faculty judgment at the center of a nationally shared set of expectations for liberal learning.
- Rubrics create a roadmap for shared learning across the curriculum and cocurriculum—from the course level to institutional reporting levels, and from general institutional or programmatic contexts to specific course contexts.

In brief, the VALUE rubrics create a frame for faculty work. We have developed the following protocol for individual faculty members to follow as they begin to use rubrics within their own campus contexts:

1. Bear in mind that a scoring rubric is an attempt to draw attention to the specific features of student work that indicate the student's performance on an academic task; thus, the rubric serves as a set of filters to help readers sort out qualities in the work itself.
2. Read through the rubric carefully, paying attention to the framing language and the glossary definitions.
3. Start with a student sample from your institution, ideally with the assignment attached.
4. Keep the elements of the rubric in mind as you read the student's work, perhaps making notes about how well the student's effort matches the described levels; if there is no match, note that as well.
5. Rate each element of the rubric, recognizing that student work may show strengths in some areas and weaknesses in others.
6. Discuss with other raters on your campus the qualities you are using to indicate particular ratings of students' work; use these discussions as the basis for developing shared definitions of important qualities.
7. Once you have finished, consider and reflect on the following questions:
   - What do you see as the assignment for this paper or portfolio?
   - When you read the rubric, what terms seemed most important to you in the criteria?
   - When you read the paper or portfolio, how did the important terms influence your reading and lead you to a score?
   - Can you write one or two sentences describing the characteristics of this paper or portfolio that led you to the score you assigned?

By focusing in a manageable way on the key criteria or characteristics of learning for each of the liberal learning outcomes, this simple protocol can help faculty approach what, to many, may seem to be a daunting task. Further, it allows the rubrics to be translated into the campus context in such a way that the results reflect the mission, goals, and students of the institution, while still nesting the results within the broader, national understanding of liberal learning and student achievement.

LINDA ADLER-KASSNER *is professor of English language and literature and director of first-year writing at Eastern Michigan University,* **CAROL RUTZ** *is director of the college writing program and senior lecturer in English at Carleton College, and* **SUSANMARIE HARRINGTON** *is director of writing in the disciplines at the University of Vermont.*

APPENDIX:

The VALUE Rubrics

As part of AAC&U's Liberal Education and America's Promise (LEAP) initiative, the VALUE (Valid Assessment of Learning in Undergraduate Education) project seeks to contribute to the national dialogue on assessment of college student learning. It builds on a philosophy of learning assessment that privileges multiple expert judgments of the quality of student work over reliance on standardized tests administered to samples of students outside of their required curriculum or cocurriculum. The assessment approaches that VALUE advances are based on the shared understanding of faculty and academic professionals on campuses from across the country.

VALUE assumes that:
- to achieve a high-quality education for all students, valid assessment data are needed to guide planning, teaching, and improvement;
- colleges and universities seek to foster and assess numerous essential learning outcomes beyond those addressed by currently available standardized tests;
- learning develops over time and should become more complex and sophisticated as students move through their curricular and cocurricular educational pathways toward a degree;
- good practice in assessment requires multiple assessments, over time; well-planned electronic portfolios provide opportunities to collect data from multiple assessments across a broad range of learning outcomes while guiding student learning and building self-assessment capabilities;
- electronic portfolios and assessment of work in them can inform programs and institutions on progress in achieving expected goals.

As part of the VALUE project, rubrics were developed by teams of faculty experts representing colleges and universities across the United States through a process that examined many existing campus rubrics and related documents for each learning outcome and incorporated additional feedback from faculty. The rubrics articulate fundamental criteria for each learning outcome, with performance descriptors demonstrating progressively more sophisticated levels of attainment. The rubrics are intended for institutional level use in evaluating and discussing student learning, not for grading. The core expectations articulated in all fifteen of the VALUE rubrics can and should be translated into the language of individual campuses, disciplines, and even courses. The utility of the VALUE rubrics is to position learning at all undergraduate levels within a basic framework of expectations such that evidence of learning can by shared nationally through a common dialog and understanding of student success.

> The VALUE rubrics reflect faculty shared expectations for essential learning across the nation regardless of type of institution, mission, size, or location.

AAC&U invites faculty and campuses to use the VALUE rubrics to engage conversations about expected student learning; to adapt and use the rubrics to assess collections of student work; and to share with us the usefulness, effectiveness, and suggestions for improvement that emerge from campus experience. Feedback can be sent to value@aacu.org.

VALUE Rubric: Inquiry and Analysis

FRAMING LANGUAGE

This rubric is designed for use in a wide variety of disciplines. Since the terminology and process of inquiry are discipline-specific, an effort has been made here to use broad language that reflects multiple approaches and assignments while addressing the fundamental elements of sound inquiry and analysis (including topic selection, knowledge, design, analysis, etc.). The language of the rubric assumes that the inquiry and analysis process is appropriate to the discipline in which the work is being done. For example, if analysis using statistical methods is appropriate to the discipline, then a student would be expected to use an appropriate statistical methodology for that analysis. If a student does not use a discipline-appropriate process, then his or her work should receive a performance rating of "1" or "0" for that criterion.

In addition, this rubric addresses the *products* of analysis and inquiry, not the *processes* themselves. The complexity of inquiry and analysis tasks is determined, in part, by how much information or guidance is provided to a student and how much the student constructs for himself or herself. The more the student constructs, the more complex the inquiry process. For this reason, while the rubric can be used when the assignments or purposes for work are unknown, it will work most effectively when those are known. Finally, faculty are encouraged to adapt the essence and language of each rubric criterion to the disciplinary or interdisciplinary context to which it is applied.

GLOSSARY

The definitions that follow were developed to clarify terms and concepts as used in this rubric only.

- Conclusions: A synthesis of key findings drawn from research/evidence.
- Limitations: Critique of the process or evidence.
- Implications: How inquiry results apply to a larger context or to the real world.

VALUE Rubric: Inquiry and Analysis

DEFINITION

The ability to know when there is a need for information, to be able to identify, locate, evaluate, and effectively and responsibly use and share that information for the problem at hand. - The National Forum on Information Literacy

Evaluators are encouraged to assign a zero to any work sample or collection of work that does not meet benchmark (cell one) level performance.

	CAPSTONE (4)	MILESTONES (3)	MILESTONES (2)	BENCHMARK (1)
Topic selection	Identifies a creative, focused, and manageable topic that addresses potentially significant yet previously less-explored aspects of the topic.	Identifies a focused and manageable/doable topic that appropriately addresses relevant aspects of the topic.	Identifies a topic that while manageable/doable, is too narrowly focused and leaves out relevant aspects of the topic.	Identifies a topic that is far too general and wide-ranging as to be manageable and doable.
Existing Knowledge, Research, and/or Views	Synthesizes in-depth information from relevant sources representing various points of view/approaches.	Presents in-depth information from relevant sources representing various points of view/approaches.	Presents information from relevant sources representing limited points of view/approaches.	Presents information from irrelevant sources representing limited points of view/approaches.
Design Process	All elements of the methodology or theoretical framework are skillfully developed. Appropriate methodology or theoretical frameworks may be synthesized from across disciplines or from relevant subdisciplines.	Critical elements of the methodology or theoretical framework are appropriately developed, however, more subtle elements are ignored or unaccounted for.	Critical elements of the methodology or theoretical framework are missing, incorrectly developed, or unfocused.	Inquiry design demonstrates a misunderstanding of the methodology or theoretical framework.
Analysis	Organizes and synthesizes evidence to reveal insightful patterns, differences, or similarities related to focus.	Organizes evidence to reveal important patterns, differences, or similarities related to focus.	Organizes evidence, but the organization is not effective in revealing important patterns, differences, or similarities.	Lists evidence, but it is not organized and/or is unrelated to focus.
Conclusions	States a conclusion that is a logical extrapolation from the inquiry findings.	States a conclusion focused solely on the inquiry findings. The conclusion arises specifically from and responds specifically to the inquiry findings.	States a general conclusion that, because it is so general, also applies beyond the scope of the inquiry findings.	States an ambiguous, illogical, or unsupportable conclusion from inquiry findings.
Limitations and Implications	Insightfully discusses in detail relevant and supported limitations and implications.	Discusses relevant and supported limitations and implications.	Presents relevant and supported limitations and implications.	Presents limitations and implications, but they are possibly irrelevant and unsupported.

A PDF of this and all VALUE Rubrics can be downloaded from www.aacu.org/value/rubrics

VALUE Rubric: Critical Thinking

FRAMING LANGUAGE

This rubric is designed to be transdisciplinary, reflecting the recognition that success in all disciplines requires habits of inquiry and analysis that share common attributes. Further, research suggests that successful critical thinkers from all disciplines increasingly need to be able to apply those habits in various and changing situations encountered in all walks of life.

This rubric is designed for use with many different types of assignments, and the suggestions here are not an exhaustive list of possibilities. Critical thinking can be demonstrated in assignments that require students to complete analyses of text, data, or issues. Assignments that cut across presentation mode might be especially useful in some fields. If insight into the process components of critical thinking (i.e., how information sources were evaluated regardless of whether they were included in the product) is important, assignments focused on student reflection might be especially illuminating.

GLOSSARY

The definitions that follow were developed to clarify terms and concepts as used in this rubric only.

- Ambiguity: Information that may be interpreted in more than one way.
- Assumptions: Ideas, conditions, or beliefs (often implicit or unstated) that are "taken for granted or accepted as true without proof." (Quoted from www.dictionary.reference.com/browse/assumptions)
- Context: The historical, ethical, political, cultural, environmental, or circumstantial settings or conditions that influence and complicate the consideration of any issues, ideas, artifacts, or events.
- Literal meaning: Interpretation of information exactly as stated. For example, "she was green with envy" would be interpreted literally to mean that her skin was green.
- Metaphor: Information that is (intended to be) interpreted in a nonliteral way. For example, "she was green with envy" is intended metaphorically to convey an intensity of emotion, not a skin color.

VALUE Rubric: Critical Thinking

DEFINITION

Critical thinking is a habit of mind characterized by the comprehensive exploration of issues, ideas, artifacts, and events before accepting or formulating an opinion or conclusion.

Evaluators are encouraged to assign a zero to any work sample or collection of work that does not meet benchmark (cell one) level performance.

	CAPSTONE (4)	MILESTONES (3)	MILESTONES (2)	BENCHMARK (1)
Explanation of Issues	Issue/problem to be considered critically is stated clearly and described comprehensively, delivering all relevant information necessary for full understanding.	Issue/problem to be considered critically is stated, described, and clarified so that understanding is not seriously impeded by omissions.	Issue/problem to be considered critically is stated but description leaves some terms undefined, ambiguities unexplored, boundaries undetermined, and/or backgrounds unknown.	Issue/problem to be considered critically is stated without clarification or description.
Evidence *Selecting and using information to investigate a point of view or conclusion*	Information is taken from source(s) with enough interpretation/evaluation to develop a comprehensive analysis or synthesis. Viewpoints of experts are questioned thoroughly.	Information is taken from source(s) with enough interpretation/evaluation to develop a coherent analysis or synthesis. Viewpoints of experts are subject to questioning.	Information is taken from source(s) with some interpretation/evaluation, but not enough to develop a coherent analysis or synthesis. Viewpoints of experts are taken as mostly fact, with little questioning.	Information is taken from source(s) without any interpretation/evaluation. Viewpoints of experts are taken as fact, without question.
Influence of Context and Assumptions	Thoroughly (systematically and methodically) analyzes own and others' assumptions and carefully evaluates the relevance of contexts when presenting a position.	Identifies own and others' assumptions and several relevant contexts when presenting a position.	Questions some assumptions. Identifies several relevant contexts when presenting a position. May be more aware of others' assumptions than one's own (or vice versa).	Shows an emerging awareness of present assumptions (sometimes labels assertions as assumptions). Begins to identify some contexts when presenting a position.
Student's Position (perspective, thesis/ hypothesis)	Specific position (perspective, thesis/ hypothesis) is imaginative, taking into account the complexities of an issue. Limits of position (perspective, thesis/ hypothesis) are acknowledged. Others' points of view are synthesized within position (perspective, thesis/ hypothesis).	Specific position (perspective, thesis/ hypothesis) takes into account the complexities of an issue. Others' points of view are acknowledged within position (perspective, thesis/ hypothesis).	Specific position (perspective, thesis/ hypothesis) acknowledges different sides of an issue.	Specific position (perspective, thesis/ hypothesis) is stated, but is simplistic and obvious.
Conclusions and Related Outcomes (implications and consequences)	Conclusions and related outcomes (consequences and implications) are logical and reflect student's informed evaluation and ability to place evidence and perspectives discussed in priority order.	Conclusion is logically tied to a range of information, including opposing viewpoints; related outcomes (consequences and implications) are identified clearly.	Conclusion is logically tied to information (because information is chosen to fit the desired conclusion); some related outcomes (consequences and implications) are identified clearly.	Conclusion is inconsistently tied to some of the information discussed; related outcomes (consequences and implications) are oversimplified.

A PDF of this and all VALUE Rubrics can be downloaded from www.aacu.org/value/rubrics

VALUE Rubric: Creative Thinking

FRAMING LANGUAGE

Creative thinking, as it is fostered within higher education, must be distinguished from less focused types of creativity such as, for example, the creativity exhibited by a small child's drawing, which stems not from an understanding of connections, but from an ignorance of boundaries. Creative thinking in higher education can only be expressed productively within a particular domain. The student must have a strong foundation in the strategies and skills of the domain in order to make connections and synthesize. While demonstrating solid knowledge of the domain's parameters, the creative thinker, at the highest levels of performance, pushes beyond those boundaries in new, unique, or atypical recombinations, uncovering or critically perceiving new syntheses and using or recognizing creative risk taking to achieve a solution.

This rubric is intended to help faculty assess creative thinking in a broad range of transdisciplinary or interdisciplinary work samples or collections of work. The rubric is made up of a set of attributes that are common to creative thinking across disciplines. Work samples or collections of work that could be assessed for creative thinking may include research papers, lab reports, musical compositions, a mathematical equation that solves a problem, a prototype design, a reflective piece about the final product of an assignment, or other academic works. The work samples or collections of work may be completed by an individual student or a group of students.

GLOSSARY

The definitions that follow were developed to clarify terms and concepts as used in this rubric only.

- Exemplar: A model or pattern to be copied or imitated (quoted from www.dictionary.reference.com/browse/exemplar).
- Domain: A field of study or activity and a sphere of knowledge and influence.

VALUE Rubric: Creative Thinking

DEFINITION

Creative thinking is both the capacity to combine or synthesize existing ideas, images, or expertise in original ways and the experience of thinking, reacting, and working in an imaginative way characterized by a high degree of innovation, divergent thinking, and risk taking.

Evaluators are encouraged to assign a zero to any work sample or collection of work that does not meet benchmark (cell one) level performance.

	CAPSTONE (4)	MILESTONES (3)	MILESTONES (2)	BENCHMARK (1)
Acquiring Competencies *This step refers to acquiring strategies and skills within a particular domain.*	Reflect: Evaluates creative process and product using domain-appropriate criteria.	Create: Creates an entirely new object, solution or idea that is appropriate to the domain.	Adapt: Successfully adapts an appropriate exemplar to his/her own specifications.	Model: Successfully reproduces an appropriate exemplar.
Taking Risks *May include personal risk (fear of embarrassment or rejection) or risk of failure in successfully completing assignment, i.e. going beyond original parameters of assignment, introducing new materials and forms, tackling controversial topics, advocating unpopular ideas or solutions.*	Actively seeks out and follows through on untested and potentially risky directions or approaches to the assignment in the final product.	Incorporates new directions or approaches to the assignment in the final product.	Considers new directions or approaches without going beyond the guidelines of the assignment.	Stays strictly within the guidelines of the assignment.
Solving Problems	Not only develops a logical, consistent plan to solve problem, but recognizes consequences of solution and can articulate reason for choosing solution.	Having selected from among alternatives, develops a logical, consistent plan to solve the problem.	Considers and rejects less acceptable approaches to solving problem.	Only a single approach is considered and is used to solve the problem.
Embracing Contradictions	Integrates alternate, divergent, or contradictory perspectives or ideas fully.	Incorporates alternate, divergent, or contradictory perspectives or ideas in a exploratory way.	Includes (recognizes the value of) alternate, divergent, or contradictory perspectives or ideas in a small way.	Acknowledges (mentions in passing) alternate, divergent, or contradictory perspectives or ideas.
Thinking Innovatively *Novelty or uniqueness (of idea, claim, question, form, etc.)*	Extends a novel or unique idea, question, format, or product to create new knowledge or knowledge that crosses boundaries.	Creates a novel or unique idea, question, format, or product.	Experiments with creating a novel or unique idea, question, format, or product.	Reformulates a collection of available ideas.
Connecting, Synthesizing, Transforming	Transforms ideas or solutions into entirely new forms.	Synthesizes ideas or solutions into a coherent whole.	Connects ideas or solutions in novel ways.	Recognizes existing connections among ideas or solutions.

A PDF of this and all VALUE Rubrics can be downloaded from www.aacu.org/value/rubrics

VALUE Rubric: Written Communication

FRAMING LANGUAGE

This writing rubric is designed for use in a wide variety of educational institutions. The most clear finding to emerge from decades of research on writing assessment is that the best writing assessments are locally determined and sensitive to local context and mission. Users of this rubric should, in the end, consider making adaptations and additions that clearly link the language of the rubric to individual campus contexts.

This rubric focuses assessment on how specific written work samples or collections of work respond to specific contexts. The central question guiding the rubric is, how well does writing respond to the needs of the audience(s) for the work? In focusing on this question, the rubric does not attend to other aspects of writing that are equally important: issues of writing process, writing strategies, the writer's fluency with different modes of textual production or publication, or the writer's growing engagement with writing and disciplinarity through the process of writing.

Evaluators using this rubric must have information about the assignments or purposes for writing that guided the writer's work. Also recommended is including reflective work samples or collections of work that address such questions as, what decisions did the writer make about audience, purpose, and genre as he or she compiled the work in the portfolio? How are those choices evident in the writing—in the content, organization and structure, reasoning, evidence, mechanical and surface conventions, and citational systems used? This will enable evaluators to have a clear sense of how writers understand the assignments and to take it into consideration as they evaluate

The first section of this rubric addresses the context and purpose for writing. A work sample or collections of work can convey the context and purpose for the writing tasks it showcases by including the writing assignments associated with work samples. But writers may also convey the context and purpose for their writing within the texts themselves. It is important for faculty and institutions to include directions for how students should represent their writing contexts and purposes.

Faculty interested in the research on writing assessment that has guided the creation of this rubric should consult the white paper on writing assessment prepared in 2008 by the National Council of Teachers of English and the Council of Writing Program Administrators (www.wpacouncil.org/whitepaper) and the position statement on writing assessment issued in 2008 by the Conference on College Composition and Communication (www.ncte.org/positions).

GLOSSARY

The definitions that follow were developed to clarify terms and concepts as used in this rubric only.

- Content development: The ways in which the text explores and represents its topic in relation to its audience and purpose.
- Context of and purpose for writing: The context of writing is the situation surrounding a text: Who is writing it? Who is reading it? Under what circumstances will the text be shared or circulated? What social or political factors might affect how the text is composed or interpreted? The purpose for writing is the writer's intended effect on an audience. Writers might want to persuade or inform; they might want to report or summarize information; they might want to work through complexity or confusion; they might want to argue or connect with other writers; they might want to convey urgency or amuse; they might write for themselves, for an assignment, or to remember.
- Disciplinary conventions: Formal and informal rules that constitute what is seen generally as appropriate within different academic fields, for example, introductory strategies, use of the passive voice or first-person point of view, expectations for thesis or hypothesis, expectations for the kinds of evidence and support that are appropriate to the task at hand, and use of primary and secondary sources to provide evidence, support arguments, or document critical perspectives on the topic. Writers will incorporate sources according to disciplinary and genre conventions, and according to the writer's purpose for the text. Through an increasingly sophisticated use of sources, writers develop the ability to differentiate between their own ideas and the ideas of others, to credit and build upon work already accomplished in the field or pertaining to the issue they are addressing, and to provide meaningful examples to readers.
- Evidence: Source material that is used to extend, in purposeful ways, writers' ideas in a text.
- Genre conventions: Formal and informal rules for particular kinds of texts or media that guide formatting, organization, and stylistic choices (e.g, lab reports, academic papers, poetry, Web pages, or personal essays).
- Sources: Texts (written, oral, behavioral, visual, or other) that writers draw on as they work for a variety of purposes, including, for example, to extend, argue with, develop, define, or shape their ideas.

VALUE Rubric: Written Communication

DEFINITION

Written communication is the development and expression of ideas in writing. Written communication involves learning to work in many genres and styles. It can involve working with many different writing technologies, and mixing texts, data, and images. Written communication abilities develop through iterative experiences across the curriculum.

Evaluators are encouraged to assign a zero to any work sample or collection of work that does not meet benchmark (cell one) level performance.

	CAPSTONE (4)	MILESTONES (3)	MILESTONES (2)	BENCHMARK (1)
Context of and Purpose for Writing *Includes considerations of audience, purpose, and the circumstances surrounding the writing task(s).*	Demonstrates a thorough understanding of context, audience, and purpose that is responsive to the assigned task(s) and focuses all elements of the work.	Demonstrates adequate consideration of context, audience, and purpose and a clear focus on the assigned task(s) (e.g., the task aligns with audience, purpose, and context).	Demonstrates awareness of context, audience, purpose, and to the assigned task(s) (e.g., begins to show awareness of audience's perceptions and assumptions).	Demonstrates minimal attention to context, audience, purpose, and to the assigned tasks(s) (e.g., expectation of instructor or self as audience).
Content Development	Uses appropriate, relevant, and compelling content to illustrate mastery of the subject, conveying the writer's understanding, and shaping the whole work.	Uses appropriate, relevant, and compelling content to explore ideas within the context of the discipline and shape the whole work.	Uses appropriate and relevant content to develop and explore ideas through most of the work.	Uses appropriate and relevant content to develop simple ideas in some parts of the work.
Genre and Disciplinary Conventions *Formal and informal rules inherent in the expectations for writing in particular forms and/or academic fields (please see glossary).*	Demonstrates detailed attention to and successful execution of a wide range of conventions particular to a specific discipline and/or writing task(s) including, organization, content, presentation, formatting, and stylistic choices	Demonstrates consistent use of important conventions particular to a specific discipline and/or writing task(s), including organization, content, presentation, and stylistic choices	Follows expectations appropriate to a specific discipline and/or writing task(s) for basic organization, content, and presentation	Attempts to use a consistent system for basic organization and presentation.
Sources and Evidence	Demonstrates skillful use of high-quality, credible, relevant sources to develop ideas that are appropriate for the discipline and genre of the writing	Demonstrates consistent use of credible, relevant sources to support ideas that are situated within the discipline and genre of the writing.	Demonstrates an attempt to use credible and/or relevant sources to support ideas that are appropriate for the discipline and genre of the writing.	Demonstrates an attempt to use sources to support ideas in the writing.
Control of Syntax and Mechanics	Uses graceful language that skillfully communicates meaning to readers with clarity and fluency, and is virtually error-free.	Uses straightforward language that generally conveys meaning to readers. The language in the portfolio has few errors.	Uses language that generally conveys meaning to readers with clarity, although writing may include some errors.	Uses language that sometimes impedes meaning because of errors in usage.

A PDF of this and all VALUE Rubrics can be downloaded from www.aacu.org/value/rubrics

VALUE Rubric: Oral Communication

The type of oral communication most likely to be included in a collection of student work is an oral presentation, which therefore is the focus for the application of this rubric.

FRAMING LANGUAGE

Oral communication takes many forms. This rubric is specifically designed to evaluate oral presentations of a single speaker at a time and is best applied to live or video-recorded presentations. For panel presentations or group presentations, it is recommended that each speaker be evaluated separately. This rubric best applies to presentations of sufficient length to convey a central message. The presentations should be purposefully organized, and one or more forms of supporting materials should be included. An oral answer to a single question not designed to be structured into a presentation does not readily apply to this rubric.

GLOSSARY

The definitions that follow were developed to clarify terms and concepts as used in this rubric only.

- Central message: The main point/thesis/"bottom line"/"take-away" of a presentation. A clear central message is easy to identify; a compelling central message is also vivid and memorable.

- Delivery techniques: Posture, gestures, eye contact, and use of the voice. Delivery techniques enhance the effectiveness of the presentation when the speaker stands and moves with authority, looks more often at the audience than at his or her speaking materials/notes, uses the voice expressively, and uses few vocal fillers ("um," "uh," "like," "you know," etc.).

- Language: Vocabulary, terminology, and sentence structure. Language that supports the effectiveness of a presentation is appropriate to the topic and audience, grammatical, clear, and free from bias. Language that enhances the effectiveness of a presentation is also vivid, imaginative, and expressive.

- Organization: The grouping and sequencing of ideas and supporting material in a presentation. An organizational pattern that supports the effectiveness of a presentation typically includes an introduction, one or more identifiable sections in the body of the speech, and a conclusion. An organizational pattern that enhances the effectiveness of the presentation reflects a purposeful choice among possible alternatives—a chronological pattern, a problem-solution pattern, an analysis-of-parts pattern, etc.—that makes it easier to follow the content of the presentation and that makes it more likely that purpose of the presentation will be accomplished.

- Supporting material: Explanations, examples, illustrations, statistics, analogies, quotations from relevant authorities, and other kinds of information or analysis that support the principal ideas of the presentation. Supporting material is generally credible when it is relevant and derived from reliable and appropriate sources. Supporting material is highly credible when it is also vivid and varied across the types listed above (e.g., a mix of examples, statistics, and references to authorities). Supporting material may also serve the purpose of establishing the speaker's credibility. For example, in presenting a creative work such as a dramatic reading of Shakespeare, supporting evidence may not advance the ideas of Shakespeare, but rather may serve to establish the speaker as a credible Shakespearean actor.

VALUE Rubric: Oral Communication

DEFINITION

Oral communication is a prepared, purposeful presentation designed to increase knowledge, to foster understanding, or to promote change in the listeners' attitudes, values, beliefs, or behaviors.

Evaluators are encouraged to assign a zero to any work sample or collection of work that does not meet benchmark (cell one) level performance.

	CAPSTONE (4)	MILESTONES (3)	MILESTONES (2)	BENCHMARK (1)
Organization	Organizational pattern (specific introduction and conclusion, sequenced material within the body, and transitions) is clearly and consistently observable and is skillful and makes the content of the presentation cohesive.	Organizational pattern (specific introduction and conclusion, sequenced material within the body, and transitions) is clearly and consistently observable within the presentation.	Organizational pattern (specific introduction and conclusion, sequenced material within the body, and transitions) is intermittently observable within the presentation.	Organizational pattern (specific introduction and conclusion, sequenced material within the body, and transitions) is not observable within the presentation.
Language	Language choices are imaginative, memorable, and compelling, and enhance the effectiveness of the presentation. Language in presentation is appropriate to audience.	Language choices are thoughtful and generally support the effectiveness of the presentation. Language in presentation is appropriate to audience.	Language choices are mundane and commonplace and partially support the effectiveness of the presentation. Language in presentation is appropriate to audience.	Language choices are unclear and minimally support the effectiveness of the presentation. Language in presentation is not appropriate to audience.
Delivery	Delivery techniques (posture, gesture, eye contact, and vocal expressiveness) make the presentation compelling, and speaker appears polished and confident.	Delivery techniques (posture, gesture, eye contact, and vocal expressiveness) make the presentation interesting, and speaker appears comfortable.	Delivery techniques (posture, gesture, eye contact, and vocal expressiveness) make the presentation understandable, and speaker appears tentative.	Delivery techniques (posture, gesture, eye contact, and vocal expressiveness) detract from the understandability of the presentation, and speaker appears uncomfortable.
Supporting Material	A variety of types of supporting materials (explanations, examples, illustrations, statistics, analogies, quotations from relevant authorities) make appropriate reference to information or analysis that significantly supports the presentation or establishes the presenter's credibility/authority on the topic.	Supporting materials (explanations, examples, illustrations, statistics, analogies, quotations from relevant authorities) make appropriate reference to information or analysis that generally supports the presentation or establishes the presenter's credibility/authority on the topic.	Supporting materials (explanations, examples, illustrations, statistics, analogies, quotations from relevant authorities) make appropriate reference to information or analysis that partially supports the presentation or establishes the presenter's credibility/authority on the topic.	Insufficient supporting materials (explanations, examples, illustrations, statistics, analogies, quotations from relevant authorities) make reference to information or analysis that minimally supports the presentation or establishes the presenter's credibility/authority on the topic.
Central Message	Central message is compelling (precisely stated, appropriately repeated, memorable, and strongly supported.)	Central message is clear and consistent with the supporting material.	Central message is basically understandable but is not often repeated and is not memorable.	Central message can be deduced, but is not explicitly stated in the presentation.

A PDF of this and all VALUE Rubrics can be downloaded from www.aacu.org/value/rubrics

VALUE Rubric: Reading

FRAMING LANGUAGE

To paraphrase Phaedrus, texts do not explain, nor answer questions about, themselves. They must be located, approached, decoded, comprehended, analyzed, interpreted, and discussed—especially complex academic texts used in college and university classrooms for purposes of learning. Historically, college professors have not considered the teaching of reading to be necessary, other than for students who may require "remediation" in this "basic skill." They have assumed that students come with the ability to read, and have placed responsibility for any absence of this ability on teachers in elementary and secondary schools.

This absence of reading instruction in higher education must, can, and will change, and this rubric marks a direction for this change. Why the change? Even the strongest, most experienced readers making the transition from high school to college have not learned what they need to know and be able to do in order to make sense of texts within the context of professional and academic scholarship—to say nothing about readers who are either not as strong or not as experienced. Also, readers mature and develop their repertoire of reading performances naturally during the undergraduate years and beyond as a consequence of meeting textual challenges. This rubric provides some initial steps toward finding ways to measure undergraduate students' progress along the continuum. Our intention in creating this rubric is to support and promote the teaching of undergraduate readers to take on increasingly higher-level concerns with texts and to read as one of "those who comprehend."

Readers, as they move beyond their undergraduate experiences, should be motivated to approach texts and respond to them with a reflective level of curiosity, and they should be able to apply aspects of the texts they approach to a variety of aspects in their lives. This rubric provides the framework for evaluating both students' developing relationships to texts and their relative success with the range of texts to which their coursework introduces them. It is likely that users of this rubric will detect that the cell boundaries are permeable, and the criteria of the rubric are, to a degree, interrelated.

GLOSSARY

The definitions that follow were developed to clarify terms and concepts as used in this rubric only.

- Analysis: The process of recognizing and using features of a text to build a more advanced understanding of the text's meaning. This might include evaluation of genre, language, tone, stated purpose, explicit or implicit logic (including flaws of reasoning), and historical context as they contribute to the meaning of a text.
- Comprehension: The extent to which a reader "gets" the text, both literally and figuratively. Accomplished and sophisticated readers will have moved from being able simply to "get" the meaning that the language of the text provides to being able to "get" the broader implications of the text, the questions it raises, and the counterarguments one might suggest in response to it. A helpful and accessible discussion of "comprehension" is found in Chapter 2 of the RAND report, *Reading for Understanding* (www.rand.org/pubs/monograph_reports/MR1465/MR1465.ch2.pdf).
- Epistemological lens: The knowledge framework a reader develops in a specific discipline as he or she moves through an academic major (e.g., essays, textbook chapters, literary works, journal articles, lab reports, grant proposals, lectures, blogs, Web pages, or literature reviews). The depth and breadth of this knowledge provides the foundation for independent and self-regulated responses to the range of texts in any discipline or field that students will encounter.
- Genre: A particular kind of "text" defined by a set of disciplinary conventions or agreements learned through participation in academic discourse. Genre governs what texts can be about, how they are structured, what to expect from them, what can be done with them, and how to use them.
- Interpretation: Determining or construing the meaning of a text or part of a text in a particular way based on textual and contextual information.
- Interpretive strategies: Purposeful approaches from different perspectives, for example, asking clarifying questions, building knowledge of the context within which a text is written, visualizing and asking questions that challenge the assumptions or claims of the text such as, what would the country be like if the Civil War had not happened?
- Multiple perspectives: Consideration of how text-based meanings might differ depending on point of view.
- Parts: Titles, headings, meaning of vocabulary from context, structure of the text, important ideas, and relationships among those ideas.
- Relationship to text: The set of expectations and intentions a reader brings to a particular text or set of texts.
- Searches intentionally for relationships: An active and highly aware quality of thinking closely related to inquiry and research.
- Takes texts apart: Discerns the level of importance or abstraction of textual elements, sees big and small pieces as parts of the whole meaning.

VALUE Rubric: Reading

DEFINITION

Reading is "the process of simultaneously extracting and constructing meaning through interaction and involvement with written language" (Snow et al., 2002). (From www.rand.org/pubs/research_briefs/RB8024/index1.html)

Evaluators are encouraged to assign a zero to any work sample or collection of work that does not meet benchmark (cell one) level performance.

	CAPSTONE (4)	MILESTONES (3)	MILESTONES (2)	BENCHMARK (1)
Comprehension	Recognizes possible implications of the text for contexts, perspectives, or issues beyond the assigned task within the classroom or beyond the author's explicit message (e.g., might recognize broader issues at play, or might pose challenges to the author's message and presentation).	Uses the text, general background knowledge, and/or specific knowledge of the author's context to draw more complex inferences about the author's message and attitude.	Evaluates how textual features (e.g., sentence and paragraph structure or tone) contribute to the author's message; draws basic inferences about context and purpose of text.	Apprehends vocabulary appropriately to paraphrase or summarize the information the text communicates.
Genres	Uses ability to identify texts within and across genres, monitoring and adjusting reading strategies and expectations based on generic nuances of particular texts.	Articulates distinctions among genres and their characteristic conventions.	Reflects on reading experiences across a variety of genres, reading both with and against the grain experimentally and intentionally.	Applies tacit genre knowledge to a variety of classroom reading assignments in productive, if unreflective, ways.
Relationship to Text *Making meanings with texts in their contexts*	Evaluates texts for scholarly significance and relevance within and across the various disciplines, evaluating them according to their contributions and consequences.	Uses texts in the context of scholarship to develop a foundation of disciplinary knowledge and to raise and explore important questions.	Engages texts with the intention and expectation of building topical and world knowledge.	Approaches texts in the context of assignments with the intention and expectation of finding right answers and learning facts and concepts to display for credit.
Analysis *Interacting with texts in parts and as wholes*	Evaluates strategies for relating ideas, text structure, or other textual features in order to build knowledge or insight within and across texts and disciplines.	Identifies relations among ideas, text structure, or other textual features, to evaluate how they support an advanced understanding of the text as a whole.	Recognizes relations among parts or aspects of a text, such as effective or ineffective arguments or literary features, in considering how these contribute to a basic understanding of the text as a whole.	Identifies aspects of a text (e.g., content, structure, or relations among ideas) as needed to respond to questions posed in assigned tasks.
Interpretation *Making sense with texts as blueprints for meaning*	Provides evidence not only that s/he can read by using an appropriate epistemological lens but that s/he can also engage in reading as part of a continuing dialogue within and beyond a discipline or a community of readers.	Articulates an understanding of the multiple ways of reading and the range of interpretive strategies particular to one's discipline(s) or in a given community of readers.	Demonstrates that s/he can read purposefully, choosing among interpretive strategies depending on the purpose of the reading.	Can identify purpose(s) for reading, relying on an external authority such as an instructor for clarification of the task.
Reader's Voice *Participating in academic discourse about texts*	Discusses texts with an independent intellectual and ethical disposition so as to further or maintain disciplinary conversations.	Elaborates on the texts (through interpretation or questioning) so as to deepen or enhance an ongoing discussion.	Discusses texts in structured conversations (such as in a classroom) in ways that contribute to a basic, shared understanding of the text.	Comments about texts in ways that preserve the author's meanings and link them to the assignment.

A PDF of this and all VALUE Rubrics can be downloaded from www.aacu.org/value/rubrics

VALUE Rubric: Quantitative Literacy

QUANTITATIVE LITERACY ACROSS THE DISCIPLINES

Current trends in general education reform demonstrate that faculty are recognizing the steadily growing importance of Quantitative Literacy (QL) in an increasingly quantitative and data-dense world. AAC&U's recent survey showed that concerns about QL skills are shared by employers, who recognize that many of today's students will need a wide range of high-level quantitative skills to complete their work responsibilities. Virtually all of today's students, regardless of career choice, will need basic QL skills such as the ability to draw information from charts, graphs, and geometric figures, and the ability to accurately complete straightforward estimations and calculations.

Preliminary efforts to find student work products that demonstrate QL skills proved a challenge in this rubric creation process. It's possible to find pages of mathematical problems, but what those problem sets don't demonstrate is whether the student was able to think about and understand the meaning of her work. It's possible to find research papers that include quantitative information, but those papers often don't provide evidence that allows the evaluator to see how much of the thinking was done by the original source (often carefully cited in the paper) and how much was done by the student herself, or whether conclusions drawn from analysis of the source material are even accurate.

Given widespread agreement about the importance of QL, it becomes incumbent on faculty to develop new kinds of assignments that give students substantive, contextualized experience in using such skills as analyzing quantitative information, representing quantitative information in appropriate forms, completing calculations to answer meaningful questions, making judgments based on quantitative data and communicating the results of that work for various purposes and audiences. As students gain experience with those skills, faculty must develop assignments that require students to create work products that reveal their thought processes and demonstrate the range of their QL skills.

This rubric provides for faculty a definition for QL and a rubric describing four levels of QL achievement that might be observed in work products within work samples or collections of work. Members of AAC&U's rubric development team for QL hope that these materials will aid in the assessment of QL – but, equally important, we hope that they will help institutions and individuals in the effort to more thoroughly embed QL across the curriculum of colleges and universities.

FRAMING LANGUAGE

This rubric has been designed for the evaluation of work that addresses quantitative literacy (QL) in a substantive way. QL is not just computation, not just the citing of someone else's data. QL is a habit of mind, a way of thinking about the world that relies on data and on the mathematical analysis of data to make connections and draw conclusions. Teaching QL requires us to design assignments that address authentic, data-based problems. Such assignments may call for the traditional written paper, but we can imagine other alternatives: a video of a PowerPoint presentation, perhaps, or a well-designed series of Web pages. In any case, a successful demonstration of QL will place the mathematical work in the context of a full and robust discussion of the underlying issues addressed by the assignment.

Finally, QL skills can be applied to a wide array of problems of varying difficulty, confounding the use of this rubric. For example, the same student might demonstrate high levels of QL achievement when working on a simplistic problem and low levels of QL achievement when working on a very complex problem. Thus, to accurately assess a students QL achievement it may be necessary to measure QL achievement within the context of problem complexity, much as is done in diving competitions where two scores are given, one for the difficulty of the dive, and the other for the skill in accomplishing the dive. In this context, that would mean giving one score for the complexity of the problem and another score for the QL achievement in solving the problem.

VALUE Rubric: Quantitative Literacy

DEFINITION

Quantitative Literacy (QL) – also known as Numeracy or Quantitative Reasoning (QR) – is a "habit of mind," competency, and comfort in working with numerical data. Individuals with strong QL skills possess the ability to reason and solve quantitative problems from a wide array of authentic contexts and everyday life situations. They understand and can create sophisticated arguments supported by quantitative evidence and they can clearly communicate those arguments in a variety of formats (using words, tables, graphs, mathematical equations, etc., as appropriate).

Evaluators are encouraged to assign a zero to any work sample or collection of work that does not meet benchmark (cell one) level performance.

	CAPSTONE (4)	MILESTONES (3)	MILESTONES (2)	BENCHMARK (1)
Interpretation *Ability to explain information presented in mathematical forms (e.g., equations, graphs, diagrams, tables, words)*	Provides accurate explanations of information presented in mathematical forms. Makes appropriate inferences based on that information. *For example, accurately explains the trend data shown in a graph and makes reasonable predictions regarding what the data suggest about future events.*	Provides accurate explanations of information presented in mathematical forms. *For instance, accurately explains the trend data shown in a graph.*	Provides somewhat accurate explanations of information presented in mathematical forms, but occasionally makes minor errors related to computations or units. *For instance, accurately explains trend data shown in a graph, but may miscalculate the slope of the trend line.*	Attempts to explain information presented in mathematical forms, but draws incorrect conclusions about what the information means. *For example, attempts to explain the trend data shown in a graph, but will frequently misinterpret the nature of that trend, perhaps by confusing positive and negative trends.*
Representation *Ability to convert relevant information into various mathematical forms (e.g., equations, graphs, diagrams, tables, words)*	Skillfully converts relevant information into an insightful mathematical portrayal in a way that contributes to a further or deeper understanding.	Competently converts relevant information into an appropriate and desired mathematical portrayal.	Completes conversion of information but resulting mathematical portrayal is only partially appropriate or accurate.	Completes conversion of information but resulting mathematical portrayal is inappropriate or inaccurate.
Calculation	Calculations attempted are essentially all successful and sufficiently comprehensive to solve the problem. Calculations are also presented elegantly (clearly, concisely, etc.).	Calculations attempted are essentially all successful and sufficiently comprehensive to solve the problem.	Calculations attempted are either unsuccessful or represent only a portion of the calculations required to comprehensively solve the problem.	Calculations are attempted but are both unsuccessful and are not comprehensive.
Application/Analysis *Ability to make judgments and draw appropriate conclusions based on the quantitative analysis of data, while recognizing the limits of this analysis*	Uses the quantitative analysis of data as the basis for deep and thoughtful judgments, drawing insightful, carefully qualified conclusions from this work.	Uses the quantitative analysis of data as the basis for competent judgments, drawing reasonable and appropriately qualified conclusions from this work.	Uses the quantitative analysis of data as the basis for workmanlike (without inspiration or nuance, ordinary) judgments, drawing plausible conclusions from this work.	Uses the quantitative analysis of data as the basis for tentative, basic judgments, although is hesitant or uncertain about drawing conclusions from this work.
Assumptions *Ability to make and evaluate important assumptions in estimation, modeling, and data analysis*	Explicitly describes assumptions and provides compelling rationale for why each assumption is appropriate. Shows awareness that confidence in final conclusions is limited by the accuracy of the assumptions.	Explicitly describes assumptions and provides compelling rationale for why assumptions are appropriate.	Explicitly describes assumptions.	Attempts to describe assumptions.
Communication *Expressing quantitative evidence in support of the argument or purpose of the work (in terms of what evidence is used and how it is formatted, presented, and contextualized)*	Uses quantitative information in connection with the argument or purpose of the work, presents it in an effective format, and explicates it with consistently high quality.	Uses quantitative information in connection with the argument or purpose of the work, though data may be presented in a less than completely effective format or some parts of the explication may be uneven.	Uses quantitative information, but does not effectively connect it to the argument or purpose of the work.	Presents an argument for which quantitative evidence is pertinent, but does not provide adequate explicit numerical support. (May use quasi-quantitative words such as "many," "few," "increasing," "small," and the like in place of actual quantities.)

A PDF of this and all VALUE Rubrics can be downloaded from www.aacu.org/value/rubrics

VALUE Rubric: Information Literacy

FRAMING LANGUAGE

This rubric is recommended for use in evaluating a collection of work, rather than a single work sample, in order fully to gauge students' information skills. Ideally, a collection of work would contain a wide variety of different types of work and might include research papers, editorials, speeches, grant proposals, marketing or business plans, PowerPoint presentations, posters, literature reviews, position papers, and argument critiques, to name a few. In addition, a description of the assignments with the instructions that initiated the student work would be vital in providing the complete context for the work. Although a student's final work must stand on its own, evidence of a student's research and information gathering processes, such as a research journal/diary, could provide further demonstration of the student's information proficiency and would be required for some criteria on this rubric.

VALUE Rubric: Information Literacy

DEFINITION

The ability to know when there is a need for information, to be able to identify, locate, evaluate, and effectively and responsibly use and share that information for the problem at hand. - The National Forum on Information Literacy

Evaluators are encouraged to assign a zero to any work sample or collection of work that does not meet benchmark (cell one) level performance.

	CAPSTONE (4)	MILESTONES (3)	MILESTONES (2)	BENCHMARK (1)
Determine the Extent of Information Needed	Effectively defines the scope of the research question or thesis. Effectively determines key concepts. Types of information (sources) selected directly relate to concepts or answer research question.	Defines the scope of the research question or thesis completely. Can determine key concepts. Types of information (sources) selected relate to concepts or answer research question.	Defines the scope of the research question or thesis incompletely (parts are missing, remains too broad or too narrow, etc.). Can determine key concepts. Types of information (sources) selected partially relate to concepts or answer research question.	Has difficulty defining the scope of the research question or thesis. Has difficulty determining key concepts. Types of information (sources) selected do not relate to concepts or answer research question.
Access the Needed Information	Accesses information using effective, well-designed search strategies and most appropriate information sources.	Accesses information using variety of search strategies and some relevant information sources. Demonstrates ability to refine search.	Accesses information using simple search strategies, retrieves information from limited and similar sources.	Accesses information randomly, retrieves information that lacks relevance and quality.
Evaluate Information and its Sources Critically	Thoroughly (systematically and methodically) analyzes own and others' assumptions and carefully evaluates the relevance of contexts when presenting a position.	Identifies own and others' assumptions and several relevant contexts when presenting a position.	Questions some assumptions. Identifies several relevant contexts when presenting a position. May be more aware of others' assumptions than one's own (or vice versa).	Shows an emerging awareness of present assumptions (sometimes labels assertions as assumptions). Begins to identify some contexts when presenting a position.
Use Information Effectively to Accomplish a Specific Purpose	Communicates, organizes, and synthesizes information from sources to fully achieve a specific purpose, with clarity and depth	Communicates, organizes, and synthesizes information from sources. Intended purpose is achieved.	Communicates and organizes information from sources. The information is not yet synthesized, so the intended purpose is not fully achieved.	Communicates information from sources. The information is fragmented and/or used inappropriately (misquoted, taken out of context, or incorrectly paraphrased, etc.), so the intended purpose is not achieved.
Access and Use Information Ethically and Legally	Students use correctly all of the following information use strategies (use of citations and references; choice of paraphrasing, summary, or quoting; using information in ways that are true to original context; distinguishing between common knowledge and ideas requiring attribution) and demonstrate a full understanding of the ethical and legal restrictions on the use of published, confidential, and/or proprietary information.	Students use correctly three of the following information use strategies (use of citations and references; choice of paraphrasing, summary, or quoting; using information in ways that are true to original context; distinguishing between common knowledge and ideas requiring attribution) and demonstrate a full understanding of the ethical and legal restrictions on the use of published, confidential, and/or proprietary information.	Students use correctly two of the following information use strategies (use of citations and references; choice of paraphrasing, summary, or quoting; using information in ways that are true to original context; distinguishing between common knowledge and ideas requiring attribution) and demonstrate a full understanding of the ethical and legal restrictions on the use of published, confidential, and/or proprietary information.	Students use correctly one of the following information use strategies (use of citations and references; choice of paraphrasing, summary, or quoting; using information in ways that are true to original context; distinguishing between common knowledge and ideas requiring attribution) and demonstrate a full understanding of the ethical and legal restrictions on the use of published, confidential, and/or proprietary information.

A PDF of this and all VALUE Rubrics can be downloaded from www.aacu.org/value/rubrics

VALUE Rubric: Teamwork

FRAMING LANGUAGE

Students participate on many different teams, in many different settings. For example, a given student may work on separate teams to complete a lab assignment, give an oral presentation, or complete a community service project. Furthermore, those with whom the student participates in each of these different teams are likely to be different. As a result, it is assumed that a work sample or collection of work that demonstrates a student's teamwork skills may include a diverse range of inputs. This rubric is designed to function across all of these different settings.

Two characteristics define the ways in which this rubric is to be used. First, the rubric is meant to assess the teamwork of an individual student, not the team as a whole. Therefore, it is possible for a student to receive high ratings, even if the team as a whole is rather flawed. Similarly, a student could receive low ratings, even if the team as a whole works fairly well. Second, this rubric is designed to measure the quality of a *process*, rather than the quality of an *end product*. As a result, work samples or collections of work will need to include some evidence of the individual's interactions within the team. The final product of the team's work (e.g., a written lab report) is insufficient, as it does not provide insight into the functioning of the team.

It is recommended that work samples or collections of work for this outcome derive from one (or more) of the following three sources: (1) students' own reflections about their contribution to a team's functioning; (2) evaluation or feedback from fellow team members about students' contributions to the team's functioning; or (3) the evaluation of an outside observer regarding students' contributions to a team's functioning. These three sources differ considerably in terms of the resource demands they place on an institution. It is recommended that institutions using this rubric consider carefully the resources they are able to allocate to the assessment of teamwork, and choose a means of compiling work samples or collections of work that best suits their priorities, needs, and abilities.

VALUE Rubric: Teamwork

DEFINITION

Teamwork is behaviors under the control of individual team members (effort they put into team tasks, their manner of interacting with others on team, and the quantity and quality of contributions they make to team discussions.)

Evaluators are encouraged to assign a zero to any work sample or collection of work that does not meet benchmark (cell one) level performance.

	CAPSTONE (4)	MILESTONES (3)	MILESTONES (2)	BENCHMARK (1)
Contributes to Team Meetings	Helps the team move forward by articulating the merits of alternative ideas or proposals.	Offers alternative solutions or courses of action that build on the ideas of others.	Offers new suggestions to advance the work of the group.	Shares ideas but does not advance the work of the group.
Facilitates the Contributions of Team Members	Engages team members in ways that facilitate their contributions to meetings by both constructively building upon or synthesizing the contributions of others as well as noticing when someone is not participating and inviting them to engage.	Engages team members in ways that facilitate their contributions to meetings by constructively building upon or synthesizing the contributions of others.	Engages team members in ways that facilitate their contributions to meetings by restating the views of other team members and/or asking questions for clarification.	Engages team members by taking turns and listening to others without interrupting.
Individual Contributions Outside of Team Meetings	Completes all assigned tasks by deadline; work accomplished is thorough, comprehensive, and advances the project. Proactively helps other team members complete their assigned tasks to a similar level of excellence.	Completes all assigned tasks by deadline; work accomplished is thorough, comprehensive, and advances the project.	Completes all assigned tasks by deadline; work accomplished advances the project.	Completes all assigned tasks by deadline.
Fosters Constructive Team Climate	Supports a constructive team climate by doing all of the following: ▪ Treats team members respectfully by being polite and constructive in communication. ▪ Uses positive vocal or written tone, facial expressions, and/or body language to convey a positive attitude about the team and its work. ▪ Motivates teammates by expressing confidence about the importance of the task and the team's ability to accomplish it. ▪ Provides assistance and/or encouragement to team members.	Supports a constructive team climate by doing any three of the following: ▪ Treats team members respectfully by being polite and constructive in communication. ▪ Uses positive vocal or written tone, facial expressions, and/or body language to convey a positive attitude about the team and its work. ▪ Motivates teammates by expressing confidence about the importance of the task and the team's ability to accomplish it. ▪ Provides assistance and/or encouragement to team members.	Supports a constructive team climate by doing any two of the following: ▪ Treats team members respectfully by being polite and constructive in communication. ▪ Uses positive vocal or written tone, facial expressions, and/or body language to convey a positive attitude about the team and its work. ▪ Motivates teammates by expressing confidence about the importance of the task and the team's ability to accomplish it. ▪ Provides assistance and/or encouragement to team members.	Supports a constructive team climate by doing any one of the following: ▪ Treats team members respectfully by being polite and constructive in communication. ▪ Uses positive vocal or written tone, facial expressions, and/or body language to convey a positive attitude about the team and its work. ▪ Motivates teammates by expressing confidence about the importance of the task and the team's ability to accomplish it. ▪ Provides assistance and/or encouragement to team members.
Responds to Conflict	Addresses destructive conflict directly and constructively, helping to manage/resolve it in a way that strengthens overall team cohesiveness and future effectiveness.	Identifies and acknowledges conflict and stays engaged with it.	Redirects focus toward common ground, toward task at hand (away from conflict).	Passively accepts alternate viewpoints/ideas/opinions.

A PDF of this and all VALUE Rubrics can be downloaded from www.aacu.org/value/rubrics

VALUE Rubric: Problem Solving

FRAMING LANGUAGE

Problem solving covers a wide range of activities that may vary significantly across disciplines. Activities that encompass problem solving by students may involve problems that range from well-defined to ambiguous in a simulated or laboratory context, or in real-world settings. This rubric distills the common elements of most problem-solving contexts and is designed to function across all disciplines. It is broad-based enough to allow for individual differences among learners, yet it is sufficiently concise and descriptive in scope to determine how well students have maximized their respective abilities to practice thinking through problems in order to reach solutions.

This rubric is designed to measure the quality of a *process*, rather than the quality of an *end product*. As a result, work samples or collections of work will need to include some evidence of the individual's thinking about a problem-solving task (e.g., reflections on the process from problem to proposed solution; steps in a problem-based learning assignment; record of think-aloud protocol used while solving a problem). The final product of an assignment that required problem resolution is insufficient without insight into the student's problem-solving process. Because the focus is on institutional level assessment, it may also be appropriate to score team projects such as those developed in capstone courses.

GLOSSARY

The definitions that follow were developed to clarify terms and concepts as used in this rubric only.

- Contextual Factors: Constraints (such as limits on cost), resources, attitudes (such as biases), and desired additional knowledge that affect how the problem can best be solved in the real-world or simulated setting.
- Critique: Involves the analysis and synthesis of a full range of perspectives.
- Feasible: Workable, in consideration of the timeframe, functionality, available resources, necessary buy-in, and limits of the assignment or task.
- "Off-the-shelf" solution: A simplistic option that is familiar from everyday experience but not tailored to the problem at hand (e.g., holding a bake sale to "save" an underfunded public library).
- Solution: An appropriate response to a challenge or a problem.
- Strategy: A plan of action or an approach designed to arrive at a solution. If the problem is derived from the need to cross a river, for example, then there may be a construction-oriented, cooperative approach (build a bridge with your community) and a personally oriented, physical approach (swim across alone). Another approach that may partially apply is a personal, physical approach for someone who doesn't know how to swim.
- Support: Specific rationale, evidence, etc. for the solution or the selection of a solution.

VALUE Rubric: Problem Solving

DEFINITION

Problem solving is the process of designing, evaluating, and implementing a strategy to answer an open-ended question or achieve a desired goal.

Evaluators are encouraged to assign a zero to any work sample or collection of work that does not meet benchmark (cell one) level performance.

	CAPSTONE (4)	MILESTONES (3)	MILESTONES (2)	BENCHMARK (1)
Define Problem	Demonstrates the ability to construct a clear and insightful problem statement with evidence of all relevant contextual factors.	Demonstrates the ability to construct a problem statement with evidence of most relevant contextual factors, and problem statement is adequately detailed.	Begins to demonstrate the ability to construct a problem statement with evidence of most relevant contextual factors, but problem statement is superficial.	Demonstrates a limited ability in identifying a problem statement or related contextual factors.
Identify Strategies	Identifies multiple approaches for solving the problem that apply within a specific context.	Identifies multiple approaches for solving the problem, only some of which apply within a specific context.	Identifies only a single approach for solving the problem that does apply within a specific context.	Identifies one or more approaches for solving the problem that do not apply within a specific context.
Propose Solutions/Hypotheses	Proposes one or more solutions/hypotheses that indicates a deep comprehension of the problem. Solution/hypotheses are sensitive to contextual factors as well as all of the following: ethical, logical, and cultural dimensions of the problem.	Proposes one or more solutions/hypotheses that indicates comprehension of the problem. Solutions/hypotheses are sensitive to contextual factors as well as one of the following: ethical, logical, or cultural dimensions of the problem.	Proposes one solution/hypothesis that is "off the shelf" rather than individually designed to address the specific contextual factors of the problem.	Proposes a solution/hypothesis that is difficult to evaluate because it is vague or only indirectly addresses the problem statement.
Evaluate Potential Solutions	Evaluation of solutions is deep and elegant (for example, contains thorough and insightful explanation) and includes, deeply and thoroughly, all of the following: considers history of problem, reviews logic/reasoning, examines feasibility of solution, and weighs impacts of solution.	Evaluation of solutions is adequate (for example, contains thorough explanation) and includes the following: considers history of problem, reviews logic/reasoning, examines feasibility of solution, and weighs impacts of solution.	Evaluation of solutions is brief (for example, explanation lacks depth) and includes the following: considers history of problem, reviews logic/reasoning, examines feasibility of solution, and weighs impacts of solution.	Evaluation of solutions is superficial (for example, contains cursory, surface level explanation) and includes the following: considers history of problem, reviews logic/reasoning, examines feasibility of solution, and weighs impacts of solution.
Implement Solution	Implements the solution in a manner that addresses thoroughly and deeply multiple contextual factors of the problem.	Implements the solution in a manner that addresses multiple contextual factors of the problem in a surface manner.	Implements the solution in a manner that addresses the problem statement but ignores relevant contextual factors.	Implements the solution in a manner that does not directly address the problem statement.
Evaluate Outcomes	Reviews results relative to the problem defined with thorough, specific considerations of need for further work.	Reviews results relative to the problem defined with some consideration of need for further work.	Reviews results in terms of the problem defined with little, if any, consideration of need for further work.	Reviews results superficially in terms of the problem defined with no consideration of need for further work

A PDF of this and all VALUE Rubrics can be downloaded from www.aacu.org/value/rubrics

VALUE Rubric: Civic Engagement

FRAMING LANGUAGE

Preparing graduates for their public lives as citizens, members of communities, and professionals in society has historically been a responsibility of higher education. Yet as a learning outcome, civic-mindedness is a complex concept. Civic learning outcomes are framed by personal identities and commitments, disciplinary frameworks and traditions, preprofessional norms and practices, and the missions and values of colleges and universities. This rubric is designed to make civic learning outcomes more explicit. Civic engagement can take many forms, from individual volunteerism to organizational involvement to electoral participation. For students, this could include community-based learning through service-learning classes, community-based research, or service within the community. Multiple representations of activities and artifacts may be utilized to assess this, such as:

- The student creates and manages a service program that engages others (such as youth or members of a neighborhood) in learning about and taking action on an issue they care about. The student also teaches and models ways of engaging others in a deliberative democracy, participating in democratic processes, and taking specific actions to affect an issue.
- The student researches, organizes, and carries out a "deliberative democracy forum" on a particular issue, one that includes multiple perspectives on that issue and considers how best to make positive change through various courses of public action. As a result, other students, faculty, and community members are engaged to take action on an issue.
- The student works on and takes a leadership role in a complex campaign to bring about tangible changes in the public's awareness of or education on a particular issue, or even a change in public policy. Through this process, the student demonstrates multiple types of civic action and skills.
- The student integrates his or her academic work with community engagement, producing a tangible product (piece of legislation or policy, a business, building or civic infrastructure, water quality or scientific assessment, needs survey, research paper, service program, or organization) that has engaged community constituents and responded to community needs and assets through the process.

In addition, the nature of this work lends itself to opening up the review process to include community constituents who may be a part of the work, such as teammates, colleagues, community or agency members, and those served by or collaborating in the process.

GLOSSARY

The definitions that follow were developed to clarify terms and concepts used in this rubric only.

- **Civic identity:** One sees oneself as an active participant in society with strong commitment and responsibility to work with others towards public purposes.
- **Service-learning class:** Course-based educational experience in which students participate in an organized service activity; reflect on the experience in such a way as to gain further understanding of course content, broader appreciation of the discipline, and enhanced sense of personal values and civic responsibility.
- **Communication skills:** Listening, deliberation, negotiation, consensus building, and productive use of conflict.
- **Civic life:** The public life of the citizen concerned with the affairs of the community and nation as contrasted with private or personal life, which is devoted to the pursuit of private and personal interests.
- **Politics:** A process by which a group of people, whose opinions or interests might be divergent, reach collective decisions that are generally regarded as binding on the group and enforced as common policy. Political life enables people to accomplish goals they could not realize as individuals. Politics necessarily arises whenever groups of people live together, since they must always reach collective decisions of one kind or another.
- **Government:** "The formal institutions of a society with the authority to make and implement binding decisions about such matters as the distribution of resources, allocation of benefits and burdens, and the management of conflicts."[1]
- **Civic/community context:** An organization, movement, campaign, or inhabited space that may be defined either in relation to a particular locality (e.g., school, national park, town, state, nation) or defined by shared identity (e.g., African American, North Carolinian, American, Republican or Democrat, refugee). In addition, contexts for civic engagement may be defined by a variety of approaches intended to benefit a person, group, or community, including community service, volunteer work, or academic work.

1 Center for Civic Education, "National Standards for Civics and Government: 9–12 Content Standards," www.civiced.org/index.php?page=912erica (accessed May 5, 2009).

VALUE Rubric: Civic Engagement

DEFINITION

Civic engagement is "working to make a difference in the civic life of our communities and developing the combination of knowledge, skills, values, and motivation to make that difference. It means promoting the quality of life in a community, through both political and non-political processes." (Excerpted from *Civic Responsibility and Higher Education*, edited by Thomas Ehrlich, published by Oryx Press, 2000, Preface, page vi.) In addition, civic engagement encompasses actions wherein individuals participate in activities of personal and public concern that are both individually life enriching and socially beneficial to the community.

Evaluators are encouraged to assign a zero to any work sample or collection of work that does not meet benchmark (cell one) level performance.

	CAPSTONE (4)	MILESTONES (3)	MILESTONES (2)	BENCHMARK (1)
Diversity of Communities and Cultures	Demonstrates evidence of adjustment in own attitudes and beliefs because of working within and learning from diversity of communities and cultures. Promotes others' engagement with diversity.	Reflects on how own attitudes and beliefs are different from those of other cultures and communities. Exhibits curiosity about what can be learned from diversity of communities and cultures.	Has awareness that own attitudes and beliefs are different from those of other cultures and communities. Exhibits little curiosity about what can be learned from diversity of communities and cultures.	Expresses attitudes and beliefs as an individual, from a one-sided view. Is indifferent or resistant to what can be learned from diversity of communities and cultures.
Analysis of Knowledge	Connects and extends knowledge (facts, theories, etc.) from one's own academic study/field/discipline to civic engagement and to one's own participation in civic life, politics, and government.	Analyzes knowledge (facts, theories, etc.) from one's own academic study/field/discipline making relevant connections to civic engagement and to one's own participation in civic life, politics, and government.	Begins to connect knowledge (facts, theories, etc.) from one's own academic study/field/discipline to civic engagement and to one's own participation in civic life, politics, and government.	Begins to identify knowledge (facts, theories, etc.) from one's own academic study/field/discipline that is relevant to civic engagement and to one's own participation in civic life, politics, and government.
Civic Identity and Commitment	Provides evidence of experience in civic-engagement activities and describes what she/he has learned about her or himself as it relates to a reinforced and clarified sense of civic identity and continued commitment to public action.	Provides evidence of experience in civic-engagement activities and describes what she/he has learned about her or himself as it relates to a growing sense of civic identity and commitment.	Evidence suggests involvement in civic-engagement activities is generated from expectations or course requirements rather than from a sense of civic identity.	Provides little evidence of her/his experience in civic-engagement activities and does not connect experiences to civic identity.
Civic Communication	Tailors communication strategies to effectively express, listen, and adapt to others to establish relationships to further civic action.	Effectively communicates in civic context, showing ability to do all of the following: express, listen, and adapt ideas and messages based on others' perspectives.	Communicates in civic context, showing ability to do more than one of the following: express, listen, and adapt ideas and messages based on others' perspectives.	Communicates in civic context, showing ability to do one of the following: express, listen, and adapt ideas and messages based on others' perspectives.
Civic Action and Reflection	Demonstrates independent experience and shows *initiative in team leadership* of complex or multiple civic engagement activities, accompanied by reflective insights or analysis about the aims and accomplishments of one's actions.	Demonstrates independent experience and *team leadership* of civic action, with reflective insights or analysis about the aims and accomplishments of one's actions.	Has clearly *participated* in civically focused actions and begins to reflect or describe how these actions may benefit individual(s) or communities.	Has *experimented* with some civic activities but shows little internalized understanding of their aims or effects and little commitment to future action.
Civic Contexts/Structures	Demonstrates ability and commitment to *collaboratively work across and within community contexts and structures to achieve a civic aim*.	Demonstrates ability and commitment to work actively *within community contexts and structures to achieve a civic aim*.	Demonstrates experience identifying intentional ways to *participate in civic contexts and structures*.	Experiments with civic contexts and structures, *tries out a few to see what fits*.

A PDF of this and all VALUE Rubrics can be downloaded from www.aacu.org/value/rubrics

VALUE Rubric: Intercultural Knowledge and Competence

FRAMING LANGUAGE

The call to integrate intercultural knowledge and competence into the heart of education is an imperative born of seeing ourselves as members of a world community, knowing that we share the future with others. Beyond mere exposure to culturally different others, the campus community requires the capacity to engage those others meaningfully, to place social justice in historical and political context, and to put culture at the core of transformative learning. The intercultural knowledge and competence rubric suggests a systematic way to measure our capacity to identify our own cultural patterns, to compare and contrast them with others, and to adapt empathically and flexibly to unfamiliar ways of being.

The levels of this rubric are informed, in part, by Milton Bennett's developmental model of intercultural sensitivity.[1] In addition, the criteria in this rubric are informed in part by Darla Deardorff's intercultural framework,[2] which is the first research-based consensus model of intercultural competence. Finally, it is important to understand that intercultural knowledge and competence are more complex than this rubric reflects. This rubric identifies six of the key components of intercultural knowledge and competence, but there are other components as identified in the Deardorff model and in other research.

GLOSSARY

The definitions that follow were developed to clarify terms and concepts as used in this rubric only.

- Culture: All knowledge and values shared by a group.
- Cultural rules and biases: Boundaries within which an individual operates in order to feel a sense of belonging to a society or group, based on the values shared by that society or group.
- Empathy: "Imaginary participation in another person's experience, including emotional and intellectual dimensions, by imagining his or her perspective (not by assuming the person's position)."[3]
- Intercultural experience: The experience of an interaction with an individual or groups of people whose culture is different from your own.
- Intercultural/cultural differences: The differences in rules, behaviors, communication, and biases based on cultural values that are different from those of one's own culture.
- Suspends judgment in valuing their interactions with culturally different others: Postpones assessment or evaluation (positive or negative) of interactions with people culturally different from oneself; disconnects from the process of automatic judgment and takes time to reflect on possibly multiple meanings.
- Worldview: The cognitive and affective lens through which people construe their experiences and make sense of the world around them.

1 Milton J. Bennett, "Towards Ethnorelativism: A Developmental Model of Intercultural Sensitivity," in *Education for the Intercultural Experience*, ed. R. M. Paige Yarmouth, (ME: Intercultural Press, 1993), 22–71.
2 Darla K. Deardorff, "The Identification and Assessment of Intercultural Competence as a Student Outcome of Internationalization," *Journal of Studies in International Education* 10, no. 3 (2006): 241–66.
3 Janet M. Bennett, "Transition Shock: Putting Culture Shock in Perspective," in *Basic Concepts of Intercultural Communication: Selected Readings*, ed. Milton J. Bennett (Yarmouth, ME: Intercultural Press, 1998), 215–24.

VALUE Rubric: Intercultural Knowledge and Competence

DEFINITION

Intercultural Knowledge and Competence is "a set of cognitive, affective, and behavioral skills and characteristics that support effective and appropriate interaction in a variety of cultural contexts." (Bennett, J. M. 2008. Transformative training: Designing programs for culture learning. In *Contemporary leadership and intercultural competence: Understanding and utilizing cultural diversity to build successful organizations*, ed. M. A. Moodian, 95-110. Thousand Oaks, CA: Sage.)

Evaluators are encouraged to assign a zero to any work sample or collection of work that does not meet benchmark (cell one) level performance.

	CAPSTONE (4)	MILESTONES (3)	MILESTONES (2)	BENCHMARK (1)
Knowledge *Cultural self-awareness*	Articulates insights into own cultural rules and biases (e.g., seeking complexity; aware of how her/his experiences have shaped these rules, and how to recognize and respond to cultural biases, resulting in a shift in self-description).	Recognizes new perspectives about own cultural rules and biases (e.g., not looking for sameness; comfortable with the complexities that new perspectives offer).	Identifies own cultural rules and biases (e.g., with a strong preference for those rules shared with own cultural group and seeks the same in others).	Shows minimal awareness of own cultural rules and biases (even those shared with own cultural group(s)) (e.g., uncomfortable with identifying possible cultural differences with others).
Knowledge *Knowledge of cultural worldview frameworks*	Demonstrates sophisticated understanding of the complexity of elements important to members of another culture in relation to its history, values, politics, communication styles, economy, or beliefs and practices.	Demonstrates adequate understanding of the complexity of elements important to members of another culture in relation to its history, values, politics, communication styles, economy, or beliefs and practices.	Demonstrates partial understanding of the complexity of elements important to members of another culture in relation to its history, values, politics, communication styles, economy, or beliefs and practices.	Demonstrates surface understanding of the complexity of elements important to members of another culture in relation to its history, values, politics, communication styles, economy, or beliefs and practices.
Skills *Empathy*	Interprets intercultural experience from the perspectives of own and more than one worldview and demonstrates ability to act in a supportive manner that recognizes the feelings of another cultural group.	Recognizes intellectual and emotional dimensions of more than one worldview and sometimes uses more than one worldview in interactions.	Identifies components of other cultural perspectives but responds in all situations with own worldview.	Views the experience of others but does so through own cultural worldview.
Skills *Verbal and nonverbal communication*	Articulates a complex understanding of cultural differences in verbal and nonverbal communication (e.g., demonstrates understanding of the degree to which people use physical contact while communicating in different cultures or use direct/indirect and explicit/implicit meanings) and is able to skillfully negotiate a shared understanding based on those differences.	Recognizes and participates in cultural differences in verbal and nonverbal communication and begins to negotiate a shared understanding based on those differences.	Identifies some cultural differences in verbal and nonverbal communication and is aware that misunderstandings can occur based on those differences but is still unable to negotiate a shared understanding.	Has a minimal level of understanding of cultural differences in verbal and nonverbal communication; is unable to negotiate a shared understanding.
Attitudes *Curiosity*	Asks complex questions about other cultures, seeks out and articulates answers to these questions that reflect multiple cultural perspectives.	Asks deeper questions about other cultures and seeks out answers to these questions.	Asks simple or surface questions about other cultures.	States minimal interest in learning more about other cultures.
Attitudes *Openness*	Initiates and develops interactions with culturally different others. Suspends judgment in valuing her/his interactions with culturally different others.	Begins to initiate and develop interactions with culturally different others. Begins to suspend judgment in valuing her/his interactions with culturally different others.	Expresses openness to most, if not all, interactions with culturally different others. Has difficulty suspending any judgment in her/his interactions with culturally different others, and is aware of own judgment and expresses a willingness to change.	Receptive to interacting with culturally different others. Has difficulty suspending any judgment in her/his interactions with culturally different others, but is unaware of own judgment.

A PDF of this and all VALUE Rubrics can be downloaded from www.aacu.org/value/rubrics

VALUE Rubric: Ethical Reasoning

FRAMING LANGUAGE

This rubric is intended to help faculty evaluate work samples and collections of work that demonstrate student learning about ethics. Although the goal of a liberal education should be to help students turn what they've learned in the classroom into action, pragmatically it would be difficult, if not impossible, to judge whether or not students would act ethically when faced with real situations requiring ethical action. What can be evaluated using a rubric is whether students have the intellectual tools to make ethical choices.

The rubric focuses on five elements: ethical self-awareness, ethical issue recognition, understanding different ethical perspectives or concepts, application of ethical principles, and evaluation of different ethical perspectives or concepts. Students' ethical self-identity evolves as they practice ethical decision-making skills and learn how to describe and analyze positions on ethical issues. Presumably, they will choose ethical actions when faced with ethical issues.

GLOSSARY

The definitions that follow were developed to clarify terms and concepts as used in this rubric only.

- Core Beliefs: Those fundamental principles that consciously or unconsciously influence one's ethical conduct and ethical thinking. Even when unacknowledged, core beliefs shape one's responses. Core beliefs can reflect one's environment, religion, culture, or training. A person may or may not choose to act on his or her core beliefs.

- Ethical perspectives/concepts: The different theoretical means through which ethical issues are analyzed, such as ethical theories (e.g., utilitarian, natural law, virtue) or ethical concepts (e.g., rights, justice, duty).

- Complex, multilayered (gray) context: The subparts or situational conditions of a scenario that bring two or more ethical dilemmas (issues) into the mix/problem/context for students to identify or discuss.

- Cross-relationships among the issues: Obvious or subtle connections between or among the subparts or situational conditions of the issues present in a scenario (e.g., the relationship between climate change and corn production).

VALUE Rubric: Ethical Reasoning

DEFINITION

Ethical Reasoning is reasoning about right and wrong human conduct. It requires students to be able to assess their own ethical values and the social context of problems, recognize ethical issues in a variety of settings, think about how different ethical perspectives might be applied to ethical dilemmas, and consider the ramifications of alternative actions. Students' ethical self-identity evolves as they practice ethical decision-making skills and learn how to describe and analyze positions on ethical issues.

Evaluators are encouraged to assign a zero to any work sample or collection of work that does not meet benchmark (cell one) level performance.

	CAPSTONE (4)	MILESTONES (3)	MILESTONES (2)	BENCHMARK (1)
Ethical Self-Awareness	Student discusses in detail/analyzes both core beliefs and the origins of the core beliefs and discussion has greater depth and clarity.	Student discusses in detail/analyzes both core beliefs and the origins of the core beliefs.	Student states both core beliefs and the origins of the core beliefs.	Student states either their core beliefs or articulates the origins of the core beliefs but not both.
Understanding Different Ethical Perspectives/Concepts	Student names the theory or theories, can present the gist of said theory or theories, and accurately explains the details of the theory or theories used.	Student can name the major theory or theories she/he uses, can present the gist of said theory or theories, and attempts to explain the details of the theory or theories used, but has some inaccuracies.	Student can name the major theory she/he uses, and is only able to present the gist of the named theory.	Student only names the major theory she/he uses.
Ethical Issue Recognition	Student can recognize ethical issues when presented in a complex, multilayered (gray) context AND can recognize cross-relationships among the issues.	Student can recognize ethical issues when issues are presented in a complex, multilayered (gray) context OR can grasp cross-relationships among the issues.	Student can recognize basic and obvious ethical issues and grasp (incompletely) the complexities or interrelationships among the issues.	Student can recognize basic and obvious ethical issues but fails to grasp complexity or interrelationships.
Application of Ethical Perspectives/Concepts	Student can independently apply ethical perspectives/concepts to an ethical question, accurately, and is able to consider full implications of the application.	Student can independently apply ethical perspectives/concepts to a new ethical question, accurately, but does not consider the specific implications of the application.	Student can apply ethical perspectives/concepts to an ethical question, independently (to a new example) and the application is inaccurate.	Student can apply ethical perspectives/concepts to an ethical question with support (using examples, in a class, in a group, or a fixed-choice setting) but is unable to apply ethical perspectives/concepts independently (to a new example).
Evaluation of Different Ethical Perspectives/Concepts	Student states a position and can state the objections to, assumptions and implications of, and can reasonably defend against the objections to, assumptions and implications of different ethical perspectives/concepts, and the student's defense is adequate and effective.	Student states a position and can state the objections to, assumptions and implications of, and respond to the objections to, assumptions and implications of different ethical perspectives/concepts, but the student's response is inadequate.	Student states a position and can state the objections to, assumptions and implications of different ethical perspectives/concepts but does not respond to them (and ultimately objections, assumptions, and implications are compartmentalized by student and do not affect student's position.)	Student states a position but cannot state the objections to and assumptions and limitations of the different perspectives/concepts.

A PDF of this and all VALUE Rubrics can be downloaded from www.aacu.org/value/rubrics

VALUE Rubric: Foundations and Skills for Lifelong Learning

FRAMING LANGUAGE

This rubric is designed to assess the skills and dispositions involved in lifelong learning, which include curiosity, transfer, independence, initiative, and reflection. Assignments that encourage students to reflect on how their work samples or collections of work demonstrate the application of these skills and dispositions provide the means for assessing students' acquisition of the foundations and skills for lifelong learning. Work samples or collections of work demonstrate what students know or are able to do, while reflections indicate what students think or feel or perceive. Student reflections provide the evaluator with a much better understanding of who students are because, through reflection, students share how they feel about or make sense of their learning experiences. The inclusion of student reflections on their work allows analysis and interpretation of the work samples or collections of work for the reader or evaluator. Reflection also allows exploration of alternatives, the consideration of future plans, and provides evidence related to students' growth and development. Perhaps the best fit for this rubric are those assignments that prompt the integration of experience beyond the classroom.

VALUE Rubric: Foundations and Skills for Lifelong Learning

DEFINITION

Lifelong learning is "all purposeful learning activity, undertaken on an ongoing basis with the aim of improving knowledge, skills and competence". An endeavor of higher education is to prepare students to be this type of learner by developing specific dispositions and skills (described in this rubric) while in school. (From The European Commission. 2000. Commission staff working paper: A memorandum on lifelong learning. Retrieved September 3, 2003, from www.see-educoop.net/ education_in/pdf/lifelong-oth-enl-t02.pdf.)

Evaluators are encouraged to assign a zero to any work sample or collection of work that does not meet benchmark (cell one) level performance.

	CAPSTONE (4)	MILESTONES (3)	MILESTONES (2)	BENCHMARK (1)
Curiosity	Explores a topic in depth, yielding a rich awareness and/or little-known information indicating intense interest in the subject.	Explores a topic in depth, yielding insight and/or information indicating interest in the subject.	Explores a topic with some evidence of depth, providing occasional insight and/or information indicating mild interest in the subject.	Explores a topic at a surface level, providing little insight and/or information beyond the very basic facts indicating low interest in the subject.
Initiative	Completes required work, generates and pursues opportunities to expand knowledge, skills, and abilities.	Completes required work, identifies and pursues opportunities to expand knowledge, skills, and abilities.	Completes required work and identifies opportunities to expand knowledge, skills, and abilities.	Completes required work.
Independence	Educational interests and pursuits exist and flourish outside classroom requirements. Knowledge and/or experiences are pursued independently.	Beyond classroom requirements, pursues substantial, additional knowledge and/or actively pursues independent educational experiences.	Beyond classroom requirements, pursues additional knowledge and/or shows interest in pursuing independent educational experiences.	Begins to look beyond classroom requirements, showing interest in pursuing knowledge independently.
Transfer	Makes explicit references to previous learning and applies in an innovative (new and creative) way that knowledge and those skills to demonstrate comprehension and performance in novel situations.	Makes references to previous learning and shows evidence of applying that knowledge and those skills to demonstrate comprehension and performance in novel situations.	Makes references to previous learning and attempts to apply that knowledge and those skills to demonstrate comprehension and performance in novel situations.	Makes vague references to previous learning but does not apply knowledge and skills to demonstrate comprehension and performance in novel situations.
Reflection	Reviews prior learning (past experiences inside and outside of the classroom) in depth to reveal significantly changed perspectives about educational and life experiences, which provide foundation for expanded knowledge, growth, and maturity over time.	Reviews prior learning (past experiences inside and outside of the classroom) in depth, revealing fully clarified meanings or indicating broader perspectives about educational or life events.	Reviews prior learning (past experiences inside and outside of the classroom) with some depth, revealing slightly clarified meanings or indicating a somewhat broader perspective about educational or life events.	Reviews prior learning (past experiences inside and outside of the classroom) at a surface level, without revealing clarified meaning or indicating a broader perspective about educational or life events.

A PDF of this and all VALUE Rubrics can be downloaded from www.aacu.org/value/rubrics

VALUE Rubric: Integrative Learning

FRAMING LANGUAGE

Fostering students' abilities to integrate learning—across courses, over time, and between campus and community life—is one of the most important goals and challenges for higher education. Initially, students connect previous learning to new classroom learning. Later, significant knowledge within individual disciplines serves as the foundation, but integrative learning goes beyond academic boundaries. Indeed, integrative experiences often occur as learners address real-world problems that are unscripted and sufficiently broad to require multiple areas of knowledge and multiple modes of inquiry, problems for which multiple solutions have been offered and that benefit from multiple perspectives. Integrative learning also involves internal changes in the learner. These internal changes, which indicate growth as a confident lifelong learner, include the ability to adapt one's intellectual skills, to contribute in a wide variety of situations, and to understand and develop individual purpose, values, and ethics. Developing students' capacities for integrative learning is central to personal success, social responsibility, and civic engagement in today's global society. Students face a rapidly changing and increasingly connected world where integrative learning becomes not just a benefit, but a necessity.

Because integrative learning is about making connections, this learning may not be as evident in traditional academic artifacts such as research papers and academic projects unless the student is, for example, prompted to draw implications for practice. These connections often surface, however, in reflective work, self-assessment, and creative endeavors of all kinds. Integrative assignments foster learning between courses or by connecting courses to experientially based work. Through integrative learning, students pull together their entire experience inside and outside of the formal classroom; thus, artificial barriers between formal study and informal or tacit learning become permeable. Integrative learning, whatever the context or source, builds upon connecting both theory and practice toward a deepened understanding.

Assignments to foster such connections and understanding could include, for example, composition papers that focus on topics from biology, economics, or history; mathematics assignments that apply mathematical tools to important issues and require written analysis to explain the implications and limitations of the mathematical treatment; or art history presentations that demonstrate aesthetic connections between selected paintings and novels. In this regard, some majors (e.g., interdisciplinary majors or problem-based field studies) seem inherently to evoke characteristics of integrative learning and result in work samples or collections of work that significantly demonstrate this outcome. However, fields of study that require accumulation of extensive and high-consensus content knowledge (such as accounting, engineering, or chemistry) also involve the kinds of complex and integrative constructions (e.g., ethical dilemmas and social consciousness) that seem to be highlighted so extensively in self-reflection in the arts and the humanities, but they may be embedded in individual performances and less evident. The key to the development of such work samples or collections of work will be in designing structures that include artifacts and reflective writing or feedback that support students' examination of their learning and give evidence that, as graduates, they will extend their integrative abilities to the challenges of personal, professional, and civic life.

GLOSSARY

The definitions that follow were developed to clarify terms and concepts as used in this rubric only.

- Academic knowledge: Disciplinary learning; learning from academic study, texts, etc.
- Content: The information conveyed in the work samples or collections of work.
- Contexts: Actual or simulated situations in which a student demonstrates learning outcomes. New and challenging contexts encourage students to stretch beyond their current frames of reference.
- Cocurriculum: A parallel component of the academic curriculum that is in addition to the formal classroom (student government, community service, residence hall activities, student organizations, etc.).
- Experience: Learning that takes place in a setting outside of the formal classroom, such as a workplace, service learning site, or internship site.
- Form: The external frameworks within which information and evidence are presented, ranging from choices for a particular work sample or collection of works (such as a research paper, PowerPoint presentation, video recording, etc.) to choices in the make-up of the e-portfolio.
- Performance: A dynamic and sustained act that brings together knowing and doing (creating a painting, solving an experimental design problem, developing a public relations strategy for a business, etc.); performance makes learning observable.
- Reflection: A metacognitive act of examining a performance in order to explore its significance and consequences.
- Self-Assessment: Describing, interpreting, and judging a performance based on stated or implied expectations followed by planning for further learning.

VALUE Rubric: Integrative Learning

DEFINITION

Integrative learning is an understanding and a disposition that a student builds across the curriculum and cocurriculum, from making simple connections among ideas and experiences to synthesizing and transferring learning to new, complex situations within and beyond the campus.

Evaluators are encouraged to assign a zero to any work sample or collection of work that does not meet benchmark (cell one) level performance.

	CAPSTONE (4)	MILESTONES (3)	MILESTONES (2)	BENCHMARK (1)
Connections to Experience *Connects relevant experience and academic knowledge*	Meaningfully **synthesizes** connections among experiences outside of the formal classroom (including life experiences and academic experiences such as internships and travel abroad) to **deepen understanding** of fields of study and to broaden own points of view.	Effectively **selects and develops** examples of life experiences, drawn from a variety of contexts (e.g., family life, artistic participation, civic involvement, work experience), to **illuminate** concepts/theories/frameworks of fields of study.	**Compares** life experiences and academic knowledge to infer differences, as well as similarities, and **acknowledges perspectives** other than own.	**Identifies** connections between life experiences and those academic texts and ideas **perceived as similar and related** to own interests.
Connections to Discipline *Sees (makes) connections across disciplines, perspectives*	Independently creates wholes out of multiple parts (synthesizes) or draws conclusions by combining examples, facts, or theories from more than one field of study or perspective.	Independently connects examples, facts, or theories from more than one field of study or perspective.	When prompted, connects examples, facts, or theories from more than one field of study or perspective.	When prompted, presents examples, facts, or theories from more than one field of study or perspective.
Transfer *Adapts and applies skills, abilities, theories, or methodologies gained in one situation to new situations*	Adapts and applies, independently, skills, abilities, theories, or methodologies gained in one situation to new situations **to solve difficult problems or explore complex issues in original ways.**	Adapts and applies skills, abilities, theories, or methodologies gained in one situation to new situations **to solve problems or explore issues.**	Uses skills, abilities, theories, or methodologies gained in one situation in a new situation **to contribute to understanding of problems or issues.**	Uses, in a basic way, skills, abilities, theories, or methodologies gained in one situation **in a new situation.**
Integrated Communication	Fulfills the assignment(s) by choosing a format, language, or graph (or other visual representation) in ways that **enhance meaning**, making clear the interdependence of language and meaning, thought, and expression.	Fulfills the assignment(s) by choosing a format, language, or graph (or other visual representation) to **explicitly connect content and form,** demonstrating awareness of purpose and audience.	Fulfills the assignment(s) by choosing a format, language, or graph (or other visual representation) that **connects in a basic way** what is being communicated (content) with how it is said (form).	Fulfills the assignment(s) (i.e. to produce an essay, a poster, a video, a PowerPoint presentation, etc.) **in an appropriate form.**
Reflection and Self-Assessment *Demonstrates a developing sense of self as a learner, building on prior experiences to respond to new and challenging contexts (may be evident in self-assessment, reflective, or creative work)*	Envisions a future self (and possibly makes plans that build on past experiences that have occurred across multiple and diverse contexts).	Evaluates changes in own learning over time, recognizing complex contextual factors (e.g., works with ambiguity and risk, deals with frustration, considers ethical frameworks).	Articulates strengths and challenges (within specific performances or events) to increase effectiveness in different contexts (through increased self-awareness).	Describes own performances with general descriptors of success and failure.

A PDF of this and all VALUE Rubrics can be downloaded from www.aacu.org/value/rubrics